TRADITIONAL BARGELLO

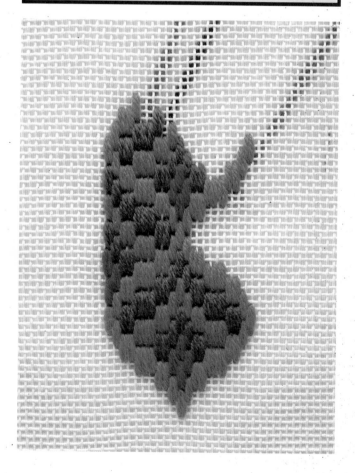

TRADITIONAL BARGELLO

Stitches, Techniques, and Dozens of Pattern and Project Ideas

Dorothy Phelan

St. Martin's Press · New York

For Brian Phelan

Library of Congress Cataloging in Publication Data

Phelan, Dorothy.
    Traditional bargello : stitches, techniques, and dozens of pattern and project ideas / Dorothy Phelan.
        p. cm
    ISBN 0–312–06882–4
    1. Canvas embroidery. 2. Canvas embroidery—Patterns. I. Title.
TT778. C3P494 1991
746.44'2—dc20

91–24895
CIP

First published in Great Britain as
Florentine Canvaswork
by B.T. Batsford, Ltd, 1991

First U.S. edition
10 9 8 7 6 5 4 3 2 1

Photoset by Deltatype Ltd,
Ellesmere Port, Cheshire
and printed in Hong Kong

Contents

Acknowledgements   6

Introduction   7

Part One: The Background and Techniques

One: Characteristics and History   12

The characteristics of Florentine canvaswork   12

The influence on Eurasian design   14

Brief history   15

Two: Stitches and Patterns   18

The naming of stitches and their descriptions   18

The patterns   25

Three: Materials and Equipment   27

Four: Preparation and Techniques   32

Choice of colour   32

Practical advice   34

Stitching   36

Part Two: The Designs and Charts

Five: Hints on using the charts   40

Good design   40
The charts   41

Six: Finishing off and blocking   93

Bibliography and notes   95
Index   96

Acknowledgements

Working on this book has been made possible by the patient indulgence of my life partner, Brian Phelan. The book is for him and for my family as an expression of my thanks. I am also grateful to my work partner Elizabeth Bradley for her forbearance. My thanks to B. T. Batsford Ltd, and my three editors, Rachel Wright, Sandra Winfield and Samantha Stead. I would also like to thank Sheila Elliott who worked out the Envelope chart for me. The samples have been stitched by Sandra Henville, Kathleen Dyson, Christine Pope, George Mabelson and Dr D. R. Wright, in addition to those I worked myself. The book would not have been possible without the assistance of these colleagues and I would like them to know how grateful I am for sharing their individual and collective skills. Special thanks to Lawrence Hopkins, Patricia Young, Angela Tomsett and Rosemary Gray. Ivan Rendall made the long stool. I would also like to mention Valerie Pitt-Rivers, Joanna Jones, Mrs J. R. Prescott and Michael Whittick.

The photographs are by Sue Atkinson of ARC studios, and I would like to thank O'Connor Brothers Ltd of Windsor for allowing us to use their showrooms for photography.

Finally, special mention must be made of Margaret Field and Nicola Gawne for extra time willingly given during my absences from The Sherborne Tapestry Centre while putting the book together.

Introduction

In 1983 my business partner Mary Elizabeth Bradley and I opened *The Sherborne Tapestry Centre*, a small needlework supplies shop in Dorset, specializing in canvas work. The decision to open a needlework shop was, for me at least, an impulsive one based on a need to 'do something' after a lifetime working in various branches of the theatre. I trained and practised as an actress, and later trained student actors. In my last years in the profession I was senior administrator and fundraiser for the Common Stock Theatre company, a co-operative which I had helped to co-found.

At first, I was unaware that childhood influences would play such an important part in my life in the shop. My father had been a talented amateur water-colourist, and my mother has had a needle in her hand, for work and for pleasure, throughout a long and productive life. As I was growing up my father encouraged me to study composition, line and colour in painting, and my mother made me aware of form, texture and stitch in embroidery – knowledge stored away almost unconsciously for future use.

The reputation of the business spread, and within three years we outgrew the original lock-up shop near Sherborne Abbey. We were then fortunate in being able to acquire the tenancy of the unique sixteenth century Listed Building and Ancient Monument in Sherborne known as 'The Julian'. With the move we were able to expand into other forms of needlework, particularly cross stitch, crewel and free form embroidery. Customers brought in their current needlework-in-process for extra supplies and frequently for advice. We were also asked to copy old, often rare, pieces on canvas, to be re-worked by the customer or professionally by us, to replace worn items. Increasingly we began to undertake the conservation, repair and reframing of other needlework. Later we charted patterns from previously worked pieces for their owners to stitch.

My interest and my knowledge have grown together. In the shop needleworkers are encouraged to discuss technical problems, and solutions evolve through consultation. Newly finished pieces are brought back for stretching, framing and making up, or simply to be admired. Needlework, especially canvas work, has become a passion with me. There is of course a great deal I can still learn. Rachel Wright, my original commissioning editor, told me that by the time I had completed this book I would know a great deal more about Florentine work. She was right. Customers have, wittingly and unwittingly, helped me in that knowledge. Needleworkers are generous and open in the sharing of their skills.

I have written the book in response to many requests for good, *new* charted designs for Florentine patterns. There have, of course, been many other books written on Florentine canvas work, incorporating many traditional designs. Unfortunately most of these are now out of print and consequently unavailable. A bibliography at the end of this book gives suggested further reading.

Many designs from one reference book are repeated with only slight variations, usually different colour combinations, in other needlework books. Traditional patterns endure because they are well designed and tested, pleasing to live with and, above all, timeless. Inigo Jones said, 'gudd manner cums by copyinge ye fairest things', but too much repetition suggests a certain stagnation and lack of current creativity. We should avoid 'the nostalgia which leads only to imitation' (Note 1).

In order for Florentine needlework to continue to survive as a vital living craft, it must join the mainstream of contemporary design. At best we can work towards an evolution in style while ensuring the continuity of the original Florentine 'brand image'. We can borrow from the new technology computer graphics, and, while acknowledging and learning from our rich needlework heritage, shouldn't we also be extending in new directions?

There are historical reasons why needlework has come to be considered only as a craft or an applied art. Rozsika Parker in her book *The Subversive Stitch* says, 'embroidery was placed lower in the artistic hierarchy because it was a collective effort associated with workers lower on the social scale than aspiring painters'. Maybe. But after all painters and needlepointers create their work on similar base media, canvas. There is a movement which sees needlework as a branch of the Fine Arts; at its best it is so, and I wish to ally myself to that movement. Certainly the prices fetched by historical pieces of needlework at recent auctions show that buyers are aware of their value. We can only hope that the skills of both contemporary professional designers and needleworkers will soon be given long overdue recognition, which should surely be reflected in the price people are willing to pay for their creativity.

Part One

THE BACKGROUND & TECHNIQUES

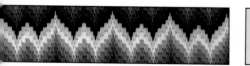

Chapter One

CHARACTERISTICS & HISTORY

The characteristics of Florentine canvaswork

Florentine work is also popularly known by the more recent name 'Bargello', derived from the set of seventeenth-century chairs upholstered in a traditional flame pattern on display in the National Museum, The Bargello in Florence. Other historical names for the work have been Irish or Byzantine.

A typical Florentine design is linear in structure, frequently, though not invariably, formed by the use of **one main establishing pattern line** repeated in different colour shading sequences throughout the piece of work. The entire grounding fabric, formerly linen but now usually 100 per cent cotton woven canvas, can be covered by the design. It is a hand-worked textile.

When the main establishing line is worked in a mirror version or inverse of itself, the design repeat becomes geometric and symmetric, and is known as Florentine-type.

Variation and movement are achieved by the subtle use of colour tones varying from light to dark, repeated in three, five, seven, nine or even more colour shades. An uneven number of shadings is always used to give a better balance and sophistication of design, and to enhance the use of shades by comparison.

The work is structured and formal, very different from free-style embroidery. This very formality and discipline give Florentine embroidery its uniqueness and richness. There are few figurative or naturalistic Florentine designs, although the patterns are sometimes used in conjunction with other styles. In *A Treasury of Embroidery Designs*, Gill Spiers and Sigrid Quemby feature a seventeenth-century valance from the Cooper-Hewitt New York collections, worked in both Florentine and crewel stitches to great effect. Another notable exception is the ubiquitous carnation design and its variations. The carnation is a favourite floral motif used in other forms of English embroidery. Reputedly a symbol of maternal love, the flower itself originated in the Far East and its name is derived from the Latin *carnis*, meaning flesh. When used in Florentine work the flower is stylized and represented by an intricate series of interlocking diamond and triangle shapes.

The present variety of stitches in all forms of needlework has evolved over hundreds of years. Stitches were borrowed and adapted from one kind of embroidery to another.

The stitches most frequently used in Florentine patterns belong to the family of straight stitches, known as 'simple satin' or 'long' stitch in other forms of embroidery. The direction of the stitches is usually vertical, and they are laid at right angles over the weft (woof) mesh of the canvas or grounding fabric, singly or in blocks. They number among the simplest and most versatile stitches in use, and have been developed from needlework stitches, such as satin stitch, which are used for surface filling.

The pattern line is followed either horizontally from selvedge to selvedge of the canvas, or diagonally up and down the canvas, always using the same group of vertical stitches. The infinite variation of stitch and step lengths used adds to the overall effect of the work.

Needlework executed in straight stitches – such as the upright Gobelin and Brick stitches, also Hungarian stitch – hangs better than fabrics worked in half cross, tent, or basketweave stitches. Straight stitches simulate most closely the weaving process used in the historical tapestry hangings such as the Unicorn Tapestries at the Cloisters Museum in New York or the Apocalypse Tapestries at Angers in France.

A variant of Florentine embroidery, Four-Way Bargello, is used most effectively and skilfully by Dorothy Kaestner in her two books (see Bibliography). In this form the north and south ground are stitched as mirror versions of each other, with the work turned first ninety degrees and then two hundred and seventy degrees to complete the east and west ground, which are in turn mirror versions of the north and south, and each other. Thus a mitred effect is achieved.

Gill Spiers and Sigrid Quemby (see Bibliography) state that the origins of Florentine needlework lie in the Brick stitch, a form of Gobelin stitch, used in much earlier medieval embroidery. (However, the word 'brick', possibly from the French *brique*, did not come into the English language until 1416.) The naming of stitches was not necessarily contemporaneous with their original use.

The influence on Eurasian design

If we accept that throughout its long history the best needlework design has been an integral part of the dominant style of any given period, we can discern in Eurasian embroidery two main streams: on the one hand the figurative, the botanical and the naturalistic, and on the other the geometric and the patterned, or abstract. I am suggesting these two main groups, over-simplified for the purpose of this book, can perhaps be traced back to the fundamental cultural differences between Christianity and Islam. Christian Art is largely representational, allegorical, didactic and story-telling, while in Islam the making of representational images was forbidden.

These two styles evolved as a result of deliberate aesthetic choices inspired by certain intellectual climates and spiritual atmospheres. They are the expression of a will, the fulfilment of a purpose.

Islamic Art is abstract and glories in making patterns by using visual balance and order which 'is far less a way of expressing an emotion than a science' (Titus Burckhardt, Foreword to Isaam El Said and Aÿse Parman *Geometric Concepts in Islamic Art*, 1976). The designs are based on the circle and its variations, which is itself an image of the 'Infinitive Whole'.

Islamic Art did not, of course, have a monopoly on the use of pattern: there was some exchange of influence between East and West.

Florentine canvas work is non-figurative, though many of the patterns are more fluid than can be understood from the terms 'linear' and 'geometric'. This fluidity is achieved by the use of colour. Curves in canvas work are an illusion because the grid of the grounding fabric is rigidly square. The shapes, usually ogees or lozenges, are made by the use of groups of stitches or single stitches worked in angular steps.

If the first influences on design in needlework can be traced to cultural, mainly religious differences as I have suggested, there is a further division which appears to be due entirely to social differences. Western royalty and aristocracy, and later the bourgeoisie, signalled their monopoly of power, wealth and status by the exotic decoration of their homes and clothes. The designs chosen were symbolic, with many references now lost. They are figurative, botanical, and stunningly beautiful. Eastern European peasants (and later the proletariat), who had little or no control over their world (and certainly less leisure time) nevertheless felt a similar urge to enhance their lives by embroidering their linen and clothes. They created objects which were functional but also gave visual pleasure. In craft design, 'Aesthetics and function are integrated and ornamentation and decoration are not divorced from utility' says Kamaladeri Chatthopadaya (Note 5). The designs used by the peasants were geometric and ordered, presented in effective and attractive combinations.

Brief history

Florentine canvas work belongs to the school of linear and geometric pattern-making. Traditionally it has been used to create beautiful textiles, for practical purposes such as bed and wall hangings in the days when rooms were draughty, and later, in a softer age, for upholstered furniture, chairs, fender-stools and footstools, as well as for smaller, personal objects such as pocket-books, wallets, boxes and needlework cases.

Reflections of Florentine design can be seen anachronistically in early western Christian ecclesiastical needlework. There are, for example, some architectural details on the Butler Bowden Cope (English 1330–50, Victoria & Albert Museum) which have patterns and shadings similar to the zigzag patterns in later Florentine work. On the German wall hanging depicting Aaron's Rod and Gideon's Fleece (1375–1400, Metropolitan Museum, New York) there are red and pink zigzag borders surrounding the entire piece accompanied by stylized five-leaf floral designs. The appliqué embroidery on the white satin cope of Mgr Freppel, Angers, depicts the saints Gregoire and Ambroise (undated in my reference) holding open books in their hands. The blue book has on its cover a design very similar to a Florentine pattern of interlocking half-circles in blues and beiges (Note 6). The techniques used for stitching are not, however, the long stitch or satin stitch associated with later work.

In the Apocalypse Tapestries (Paris 1375–80) in Angers, France, the shadings of colour and the patterns on the wings of angels (notably St Michael, whose sword resembles a rising flame), the wings of fabulous animals and the flames of purgatory are all forerunners of Florentine work. Landscape shapes in the Angevine tapestries are also represented by bands of colour shading lying both horizontally and diagonally, as do the elements fire and water, and it cannot be coincidental that Florentine canvas work has both fire and water stitch names.

The *Shorter Oxford English Dictionary* defines 'florence' as a woven fabric of wool (1483) and 'florentine' as a textile fabric of silk or wool (1545). *Le Petit Littré* (Gallimard Hachette) defines 'florentine' as a silk taffeta fabric – a useful definition, reminding us of the watered effect of taffeta, and a description which could also apply to Florentine embroidery. However, Fernand Braudel in *Capitalism and Material Life 1400–1800* (Fontana/Collins) warns us that 'many of the expressions that have come down to us did not always designate the same product and sometimes designated products which we cannot identify reliably'. I am proposing that the term 'Florentine work' and the names of some of the stitches used in this type of needlework are more than likely derived from an imitation of those fabrics in early production, and could moreover bear a resemblance to those early textiles. In addition, it can be assumed that the names signify the origin of the work. This hypothesis seems more reliable than the various legends concerning the origins of the work such as that of an Hungarian princess who married a Medici and brought in her trousseau several items embroidered in this type of stitching (surely too neat an explanation).

So, according to the Oxford dictionary the textile was established by the end of the fifteenth century and the beginning of the sixteenth century. The sixteenth century was the great age of pattern-making, according to Lanto Synge in his *Book of Needlework and Embroidery*, and this was the period when Florentine designs came into their own, influenced by the trading contacts Italy had through her great east-facing ports.

The designs draw their inspiration partly from contact with those of the Islamic empire and partly from the distinctive shapes of the Italian landscape and architecture. Italian needleworkers must surely have been influenced by the impressive order imposed since Roman, and maybe even Etruscan, times by the methodical working of the land. The terracing is horizontal, interspersed by the careful planting of trees and the siting of buildings which emphasize the vertical. These shapes are all reflected in the design of needlework patterns. It appears that it was Italian needleworkers in the sixteenth century who first set the trend for the popularity of the work which was in great demand and purchased by wealthy clients all over Europe. Florentine designs were exported from Italy, west into France through Aigue-Mortes and Lyon by the great axial routes and northwards into the Low Countries and England.

At the Chateau de Talcy, taken in 1520 by Bernard Salviati, a Florentine cousin of Catherine de Medici, there are chairs, bed-hangings and cushions covered with Hungarian point.

In the 1580s the French queen Catherine de Medici, originally a Florentine, employed the services of the Venetian designer Federico Vinicolo. Vinicolo produced pattern books favoured by needleworkers and Catherine de Medici is said to have worked some of her embroidery in the 'Florentine' style.

Fernand Braudel mentions that parquet flooring appeared in France in the fourteenth century, but only became fashionable in the seventeenth century with many variations, bonded parquets, inlaid in 'Hungarian points'. It is not known whether the stitch-name or the woodworking name came first.

The bed and wall hangings of the seventeenth century were sometimes worked in strips of Florentine stitched linen canvas joined together. The style continued its popularity well into the eighteenth century, when chairs were first padded and upholstered. There are many fine examples to be seen in houses and museums in both the UK and the USA. The North American needleworkers took the traditional patterns from Europe, adapted and extended them to their own unmistakable style. There is a Queen Anne wing chair from about 1725 upholstered in flame stitch at the Metropolitan Museum in New York. A maple and mahogany wing chair, also upholstered in the original flame stitch embroidery from c. 1760, can be seen at the Bayou Bend collection in the Museum of Fine Arts at Houston, Texas, and a further example of a Florentine embroidered 4:2 step flame and carnation pattern is to be seen at Ashley House, Deerfield. At the Henry Francis du Pont Winterthur Museum there is an Irish stitch pocket book dated 1753, and a Rococo stitch worked pocket book dated 1774.

There is a photograph of a pocket book worked by Ruth Twitchel in the year 1793 on canvas with a flame pattern in Aldoph S. Cavallo's book *Needlework* (Smithsonian Institute, 1979). This pocket book is at the Museum of Fine Arts, Boston, USA, and though it was worked forty years later than the Irish stitch pocket book mentioned earlier, the Florentine designs are almost identical.

By the nineteenth century European and North American linen samplers incorporated patterns in ogee, zigzag and half-circles interlacing. Some of these are Berlin Work samplers (popular from c. 1830–70) and show many tantalizing snatches of Florentine-type patterns, although the popularity of the work was now in decline. There is a wonderful English needlepoint rug (1850) signed M. L. Wilson, shown by Gallery Zadah, a London needlepoint carpet specialist, which has a border of triangular motifs of Florentine work, although the main pattern has a floral inner panel and an Antioch mosaic type falling cube pattern. In the twentieth century there have been attempts to revive Florentine work, but the designs seem to have lost their earlier spontaneity by pedestrian repetition. Slavishly copied patterns can become moribund.

During the 1950s, 1960s and 1970s suggestions were made for working Florentine type strips on aprons, traycloths and waste-paper baskets, but these have a certain banality. The real glory of the work is better appreciated when the object to be covered is say, a piece of furniture with the upholstered part entirely patterned, and the design given free rein.

The patterns need looking at with fresh eyes. This book is an attempt to encourage new directions that will take us into the 1990s and beyond. Once you have understood the structure of the pattern and how a different length of stitch, or number of stitches, in a block can alter the line of a curve and how the use of colour affects a design, you will want to experiment for yourself.

Chapter Two

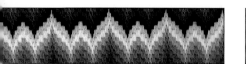

STITCHES & PATTERNS

The naming of stitches and their descriptions

As has already been said, early silk and woollen Florentine woven textiles were imported from Italy into Britain from the 1600s onwards. These sumptuous, expensive fabrics were copied by professional, and doubtless also by amateur, needleworkers. The technique was originally known as *Irish work*, and was possibly brought into England by nuns who had learned the technique in either Italy or France. Alternative names are *Byzantine* and *Bargello*. There is quite a lot of inconsistency in the stitch names, probably as a result of incorrect translation from one language to another, so I have simplified the stitch names in this book.

Diagram 1 shows *Hungarian stitch* in four forms. All stitches are worked over the horizontal mesh of the canvas. In each form all stitches touch each other.

1a.   **Hungarian stitch** used as grounding (only one colour is used: the second colour is for explanation only).

Work in horizontal rows, one row encroaching on the next.

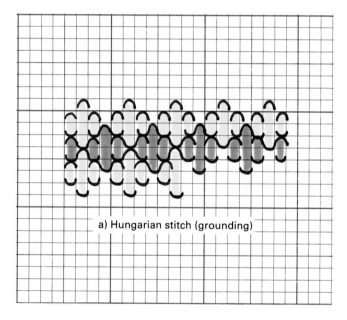

a) Hungarian stitch (grounding)

Stitch in blocks of three: one short stitch (over two threads) one long stitch (over four threads) and one short stitch (over two threads). Leave two vertical threads bare and repeat the three stitch sequence. In the second row, the long stitch is set exactly in the middle between the two blocks of stitches.

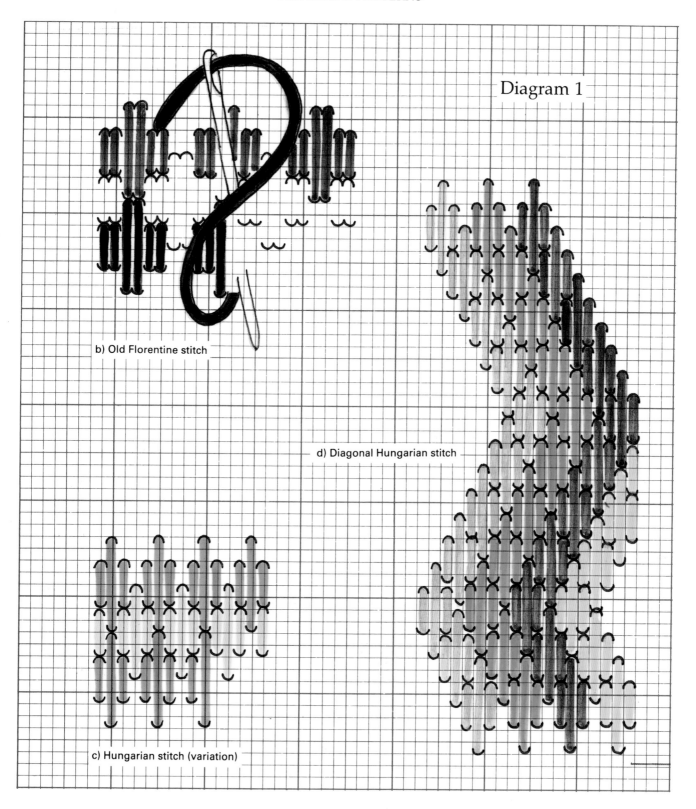

Diagram 1

b) Old Florentine stitch

d) Diagonal Hungarian stitch

c) Hungarian stitch (variation)

1b. Old Florentine stitch is a variation of Hungarian stitch. Worked in groups of six stitches, it comprises two short stitches (four threads long) two long stitches (eight threads) and two short stitches (four threads). Leave *three* vertical threads bare and repeat the sequence. The second row long stitches fit exactly in between the two blocks of stitches on the previous row.

1c. Hungarian stitch variation shows the stitch length increased in size to one short stitch (four threads long) one long stitch (eight threads long) one short stitch (four threads). Leave two vertical threads bare and repeat the sequence.

(**NB** This stitch will *not* work over three threads for the short stitches and six for the long.)

1d. Diagonal Hungarian stitch. Work the first block of three stitches as in diagram 1c above (that is, one short stitch (four threads long), one long (eight threads) and one short (four threads)). To make the next block of three stitches, repeat the first short stitch immediately *below* the final short stitch of the previous block, followed by one long stitch and one short stitch as before.

To check the pattern sequence is correct, every other vertical row of the canvas mesh should be filled by short stitches and the vertical rows between by long stitches.

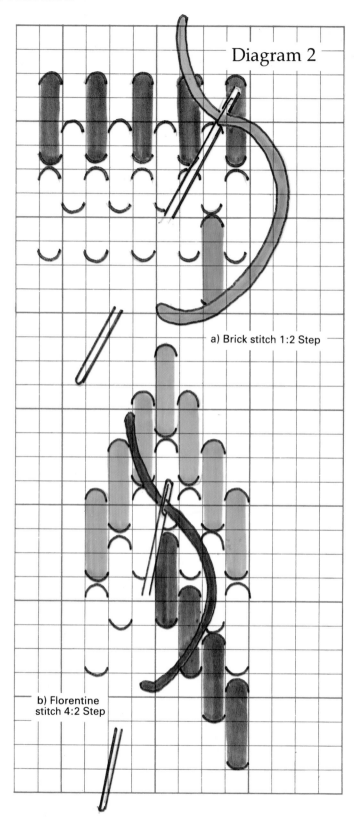

Diagram 2

a) Brick stitch 1:2 Step

b) Florentine stitch 4:2 Step

Diagram 2 shows another version of diagonal Hungarian stitch.

2a. **Brick stitch** is shown for reference only and is not used in any of the charts in this book. It is shown merely to demonstrate its probable evolution to Florentine stitch.

2b. **Florentine stitch** (also known as Irish stitch and later as Berlin stitch) is the stitch used to make the flame patterns. It is a sequence of stitches laid on the canvas mesh side by side in blocks, or singly up and down the canvas, in a regularly shaped design.

One colour sequence usually follows through the canvas as the main establishing pattern line.

The depth (or drop) of a step will vary the steepness of the incline of the pattern, as also will the number of stitches in each block.

A six-thread stitch length is the limit on #10, #11, #12 and #13 mesh canvas, as a longer stitch may catch on the finished item.

3. **Gobelin stitch** is used in the cushion cover Chart 3 and is shown in diagram 3. Each stitch is worked side by side in horizontal rows. The stitch length and step length may both vary within a row.

4. **Tent stitch** (diagram 4) is used as a making-up guideline stitch only. It looks like a half cross stitch on the right side of the work, but you should take the longest journey from stitch to stitch. The back of the stitch is also diagonal not vertical as in half-cross stitch.

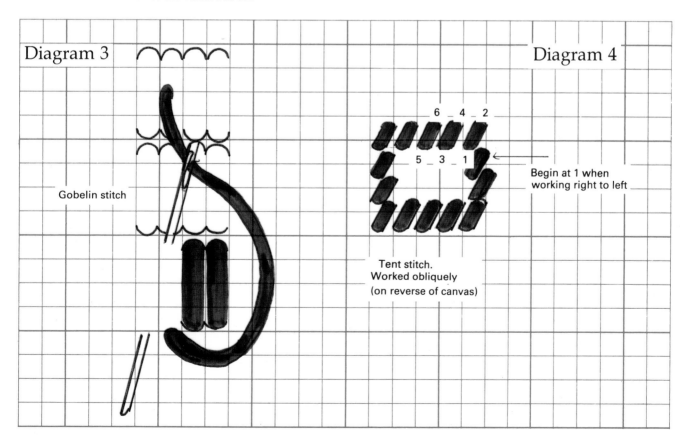

Diagram 3

Gobelin stitch

Diagram 4

6 _ 4 _ 2

5 _ 3 _ 1

Begin at 1 when working right to left

Tent stitch.
Worked obliquely
(on reverse of canvas)

5. **Hungarian point** (see diagrams 5a & 5b). This stitch sequence is worked obliquely up and down the canvas, and consists of one or more long stitches followed by two, three or four short stitches, and repeated. There is always *one main establishing line*, followed by subsequent rows which vary slightly, but logically, to make the pattern work. There is a direct relationship between the number of rows to be worked, and the number of stitches in each sequence before the pattern repeats itself. For example in a one long, two short pattern sequence, the fourth row will repeat the first. In a one long, three short stitch sequence, the fifth row will repeat the first. Once you have discerned the logic the pattern will make sense. The design fits into itself like Chinese boxes.

The following three points will help you check that the pattern sequence is being followed correctly:

1. The *vertical* lines of the pattern repeat should each show a repetition of the main establishing line (see diagram 5b).

2. Each stitch in sequence must share its upper-limit canvas mesh thread with the previously worked stitch. This is crucial.

3. Each stitch taken throughout the sequence must *move* one mesh to the left when being worked left of centre, or to the right when being worked right of centre.

Remembering these rules will help you decide whether the next stitch in sequence should be long or short.

These stitch sequences are among the most difficult of the Florentine patterns to work, and are best tackled after the other easier stitches have been mastered. But once achieved they are among the most satisfying to accomplish. After a time, secondary patterns will appear on the canvas.

1. In diagrams 5a and 5b the main establishing line is marked 1 in red and should be completed across the work first.

2. The following rows are worked in sequence, beginning with **2** up to row **4**, followed by rows **B** to **D**; then repeat the entire sequence.

3. Notice how *each* stitch shares one of the same horizontal (weft) or woof threads with its immediate neighbour.

4. Although each vertical (warp) thread marked thus * read downwards repeats the main establishing line sequence (marked in red and numbered **1** on diagrams 5a and 5b of length of stitch), it will *not be in the same colour thread* as the main establishing line.

To practise Hungarian point, fill in the left side of diagram 5a in pencil and turn the page to check your accuracy.

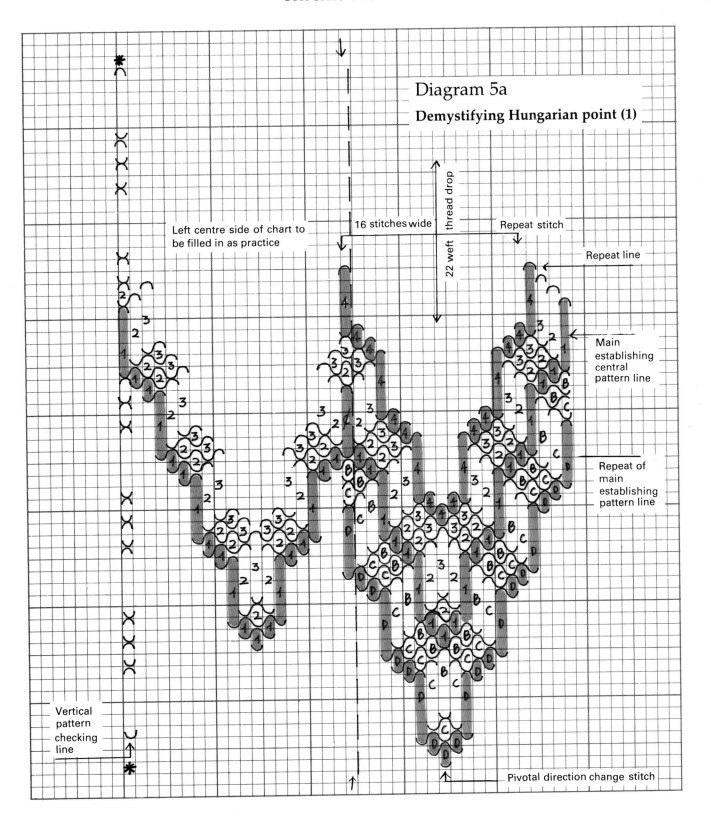

Diagram 5a

Demystifying Hungarian point (1)

Left centre side of chart to be filled in as practice

16 stitches wide

thread drop

22 weft

Repeat stitch

Repeat line

Main establishing central pattern line

Repeat of main establishing pattern line

Vertical pattern checking line

Pivotal direction change stitch

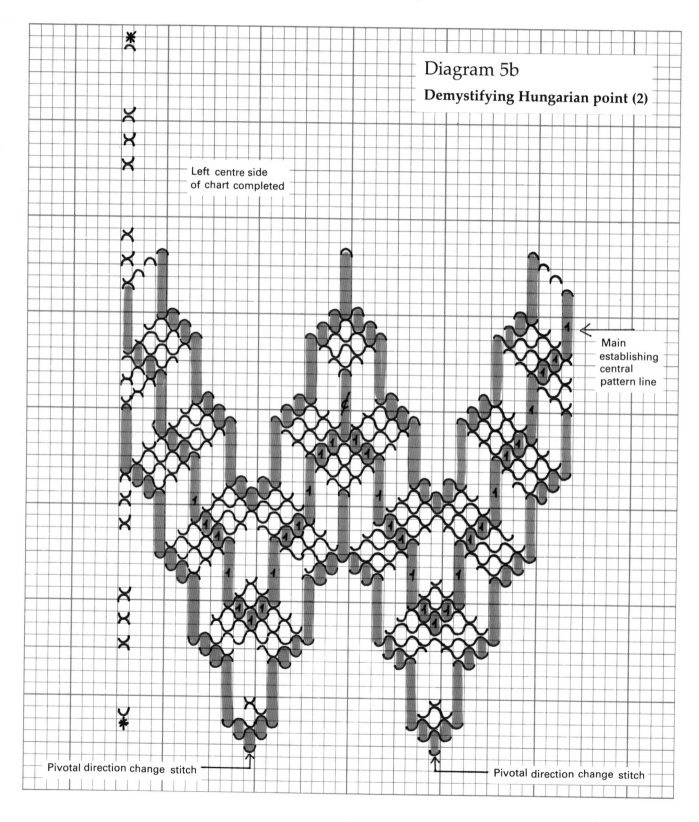

Diagram 5b

Demystifying Hungarian point (2)

Left centre side
of chart completed

Main
establishing
central
pattern line

Pivotal direction change stitch

Pivotal direction change stitch

The patterns

'It is the systematic arrangement of the repeat unit which produces the overall design.'

When a surface is to be decorated, one of its sides is divided equally into a number of parts corresponding to the number of repeat units required (*Geometric Concepts in Islamic Art*). The traditional Florentine patterns can be broken down into various elements.

Barbara Snook, in *Florentine Canvas Embroidery* (Batsford, 1967), analysed the number of stitches in each step, 'the size of each stitch' and 'the length or drop of each step'. The variations are infinite. Once you have grasped the basic principles, you will want to combine them in original ways to make your own designs. A *step*, as defined for Florentine work, denotes the number of canvas meshes jumped from the completion of one stitch up or down to the beginning of the next stitch in sequence (see diagram 6).

Do copy some of the old designs: they still have their place and it would be a pity to lose them from our vocabulary entirely.

I have also tried to indicate new directions so that your embroidery should reflect design today.

Choose a pattern which will enhance the piece of furniture to be upholstered or the place where the embroidery will sit. If the furniture is made from wood, choose colours that will complement its colour. Both patterns and colour are crucial, but *choose the pattern shape first*.

When considering a design suitable for a large object like a rug, a wall hanging, a fender stool, a window-seat covering or a chair, choose a pattern that has a large spread both horizontally and vertically over its area. For smaller objects, choose a small design which has the opportunity to repeat

itself at least three times, because the success of the work depends on the inevitability of the pattern repeat.

The patterns in the book have been arranged in skill levels ranging from one (the simplest) to three (the most complex). Patterns formed by using the same length of stitch and the same step-length, for

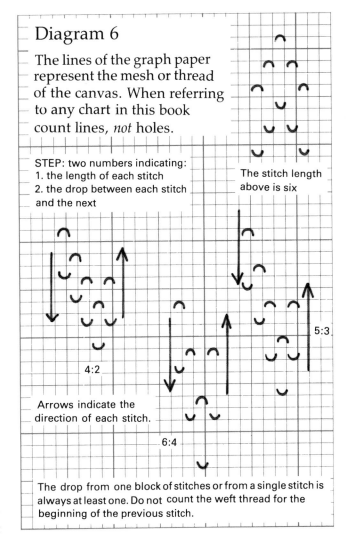

Diagram 6

The lines of the graph paper represent the mesh or thread of the canvas. When referring to any chart in this book count lines, *not* holes.

STEP: two numbers indicating:
1. the length of each stitch
2. the drop between each stitch and the next

The stitch length above is six

4:2

5:3

6:4

Arrows indicate the direction of each stitch.

The drop from one block of stitches or from a single stitch is always at least one. Do not count the weft thread for the beginning of the previous stitch.

example the simple zigzag, are best for beginners, including the very young. More advanced designs are where the stitch length and step length vary, through to the most difficult Hungarian point pieces, which you should attempt only after you have worked several other patterns with confidence.

Obviously any of the patterns in the book can be used with your own choice of colours, but take time to analyse which tones have been used in the charts. If you follow similar light, medium and dark tones to those indicated on the charts, you will achieve a similar effect. If you alter the position of the tones, the effect will change the balance of the design quite drastically. Do experiment for yourself. Remember: time and effort can be wasted on work that lacks planning and judgement.

Chapter Three

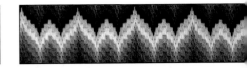

MATERIALS & EQUIPMENT

Much of the information in this chapter can also be used as a guide for other forms of canvas work. *Do plan each project carefully*. Time spent before stitching in considering the most suitable pattern for the intended purpose and the most interesting colour combination will pay off handsomely – somebody, if not you, may have to live with the completed piece for many years. *Buy the best materials available*.

Canvas

Canvas comes mainly in two widths: 100cm and 68cm (40in and 27in). It is also available in 150cm (60in) widths for larger projects. When estimating the amount of canvas you will need, first consider which standard width is more economical for your needs. As a rough guide, 50cm (20in) of a 100cm (40in) wide canvas will accommodate two cushion covers of about 40cm (16in) square, and turnings. Always add *at least* 5cm (2in) extra all round the work for these turnings, which will not be embroidered.

The selvedge of the canvas should, ideally, run up either side of the work, left and right, as the stitches sit better when worked on the correct direction of the canvas. Choose white mono de luxe Zweigart (German) 100% cotton canvas for pale and pastel shades, and ecru (natural colour) mono de luxe for dark colours. Some needleworkers prefer always to use white canvas, as they find it easier to work on because the threads show up better while stitching.

Interlock canvas, where the threads are fused together at the intersection of warp and weft, is a more rigid grounding fabric, but as a consequence the mesh tends to show through the completed work. This type of canvas is *not* recommended for Florentine work.

Penelope canvas has unequally spaced double threads which have to be separated as each stitch is worked, and should also be avoided. This canvas is used for needlework that is trammed (where the design to be worked is indicated on the canvas by basting stitches worked between the horizontal parallel mesh). It creates an unnecessary complication in Florentine work.

Check for flaws before you make your purchase. The canvas may feel stiff and inflexible at first, but this is because of the sizing applied to give it body. The canvas will soften as you work.

PVC canvas is a rigid plastic canvas available in cut sheets or, occasionally, by the metre. It comes in white and some other pastel colours, in mesh sizes #10 or #7. Use a high bulk quality yarn like knitting acrylic, which will cover the PVC better than will tapestry yarns. It is useful for teaching purposes and has the additional quality of keeping its shape so that it will not need blocking.

If the project is a straightforward, regularly shaped piece such as a cushion cover, church kneeler, firescreen, stool cover or rug, make a turning allowance of at least 5cm (2in) around the outside perimeter of the shape to be stitched. Where an irregular shape is needed, for a chair or window-seat, cut an accurate template to size in brown paper or spare wallpaper, and take it with you when buying the canvas. If you are unsure about making your own template, ask either an upholsterer or your needlework specialist retailer to make one for you. If the seat cover is a wrap-round or a covering for an entire chair, you will of course need to take the chair with you. If the seat is a drop-in, take that part only.

No. of threads in design	Gauge	Answer converted to centimetres	Design size
32×24	÷ 6	=5.34+6.00×2.5	=13.35cm×15cm
32×24	÷ 8	=4.00+3.00×2.5	=10.00cm×7.5cm
32×24	÷ 10	=3.20+2.40×2.5	=8.00cm×6cm
32×24	÷ 12	=2.66+2.00×2.5	=6.65cm×5cm
32×24	÷ 14	=2.29+1.71×2.5	=5.72cm×4.28cm
32×24	÷ 15	=2.13+1.60×2.5	=5.33cm×4cm
32×24	÷ 18	=1.78+1.33×2.5	=4.45cm×3.33cm
32×24	÷ 22	=1.45+1.09×2.5	=3.62cm×2.72cm

Diagram 7

How to calculate design size on a different canvas mesh gauge from a chart

If the graph paper does not scale with the chosen canvas mesh, count the number of threads in each direction (width and length) on the chart. Divide each number of threads per 2.5cm (1in) on the chosen canvas size: and multiply by 2.5 to calculate new design area

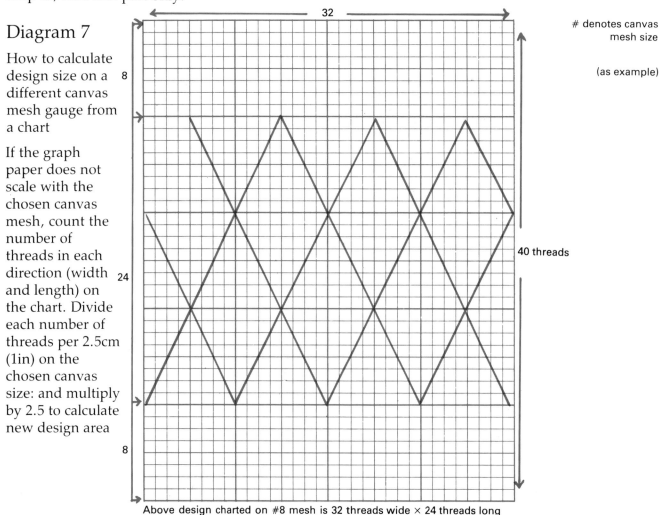

# denotes canvas mesh size

(as example)

32

8

24

8

40 threads

Above design charted on #8 mesh is 32 threads wide × 24 threads long

28

The most common mistake made by beginners is not to leave sufficient unworked canvas for the stretching (blocking) and final making-up stages of a project. I have frequently seen canvas covered completely by stitches up to 0.62cm (¼in) from the edges. This means that the stitches nearest to the outside edges of the work will be wasted, as blocking tacks and seams will encroach on them.

Choice of threads

The gauge of the canvas mesh will determine which threads you need to use to cover the canvas completely. Refer to Table 1 as a guide in making your choice; it is also useful to work a test piece for yourself before making a final decision.

Table 1: Number of strands of yarn, and needle size, needed for different gauge canvas mesh

Yarn	Canvas mesh size	No. of strands	Needle size
Appleton's crewel wool	#10 12–14 15–16 18 22–24	5 4 3 2–1 1	18 20 22 24 26
Appleton's tapestry wools	11–15	1	20–22
Anchor tapisserie and DMC wools	11–16	1	20
Paternayan	10–12 13–14 15–18	3 2 1	18 20 22
DMC Medici Wool	18 22–24	1 2	24 22

Embroidery satisfies our tactile sense as well as our visual and aesthetic senses. Most needleworkers seem to prefer a particular thread, usually either wool or cotton. All the charts in the book can be stitched in any of the yarns currently available, but you will need to change the canvas size to suit.

Consider the use to which the finished article will be put.

Wool yarn is moth-proofed and colour fast; it will wear longer than cotton or silk (in that order). Large rugs or wall hangings, for example, demand larger mesh canvas (#10 – 7) and double tapisserie wool yarn or soft cotton.

Soft cotton (DMC Retors à broder) is useful for needleworkers allergic to wool yarn. A matt thread, reasonably hard wearing, it does not rub and is useful for teaching young children needle-point techniques.

Soudan-type worsted wool is no longer available from DMC, but a similar thread is sometimes available at carpet weaving factories (such as Wilton, Wiltshire UK). It is a high bulk yarn and can be used in needlepoint rug making. It is sold cut into thrums, and it is wise to buy sufficient quantities to complete the project before you begin work, as dye lots differ and colours are often not repeatable.

Appleton Old English crewel wool, available in the UK and from specialist shops in USA, is a two-ply yarn which will adapt to the needs of most canvas by the addition of up to five strands in the needle.

Appleton Old English tapestry wool, a single four-ply yarn, can be used alone or in conjunction with their crewel wool. The wool is available in skeins (25g) and 1oz hanks. There is a wide colour range, with up to nine tones of many of the colours, which allows for great subtlety of shading. The thickness of the crewel wool is not consistent, and care should be taken to cut away any length which is too thin, as this will show up on the completed piece.

Anchor and DMC tapisserie wools, available in 10m and 8m skeins respectively, are four-ply yarns, useful in single threads. Either will sit happily with Appleton's tapestry wool. Each has good runs of colour tones.

Paternayan (Paterna), a two-ply worsted Persian yarn with three separable strands, has wide application. It comes in an acrylic colour range specially suited for use where the light is strong, and is a good quality wool. Available in skeins or 4oz hanks. For all large projects, wool purchased in hanks is more economical. Gauge about six skeins to one ounce. As a very rough guide, a stretched-out hand will cover 1oz worth of wool on the canvas.

Other yarns

DMC and Anchor (Bates) 6-stranded cottons are less durable than wool but have the advantage of a bright sheen and are suitable for canvas meshes #18 and #15.

Perlé cotton (Coton perlé) is a brilliant single stranded twisted thread with the additional quality of a slightly tougher, thicker texture than stranded cotton. Special care needs to be taken when stitching with this thread, but it goes well with any of the woollen yarns, where it can be used as a highlight.

100% silk yarn, especially the English *Designer Silks range*, is available in various weights, and in single or rainbow variegated colours. This range has a special 'tapestry' weight which can also be used very effectively for highlighting wool yarn. Silk wears least well of all yarns, but is the most pleasing to use. Expensive, it is recommended for small, luxury articles not subject to hard wear.

In Florentine work it is less crucial than in other forms of canvas embroidery to buy all the same dye lot unless you are only using one colour for a monochrome project. Different dye lots are indicated in the *DMC thread range* by slightly different labels (usually in the printing size of the yarn number), so choose skeins with similar labels if the same colour *is* essential.

Gauging the approximate amount of thread necessary for a piece of work

Different stitches and the *method* of stitching will determine the quantities needed. I prefer to cover the canvas back and front with yarn; others may choose to cover only the 'right' side of the work. The advantage of covering both sides of the canvas is that you will get greater durability. If the finished fabric is to be used to upholster furniture or withstand hard wear, do cover the back well. Worked pieces for firescreens, pole screens or decorative pictures may be sparsely covered at the back, as they are normally glazed when framed.

Needles

For canvas work, choose tapestry needles. These are blunt ended, large eyed and do not damage the canvas. They also do not split those stitches already worked. The sizes range from 13–24: the larger the needle number, the finer the needle (for example size 13 is the most coarse, and is used for making rugs).

Buy a mixed needle pack to choose the one best suited to your thread and stitches. The eye of the needle should be just large enough to take the thread easily. Care should be given to the way the needle moves up and down through the canvas mesh. If it enlarges or distorts the hole, use a smaller needle. On a complicated piece of work, thread each colour on a separate needle and pull all threaded needles not in immediate use through to the front of the work while working in another colour. This practice will avoid catching any yarn unnecessarily.

Scissors

Embroidery scissors are small and stubbier than sewing scissors. Buy the best hot tempered steel quality you can afford, and attach them to a ribbon long enough to hang round your neck when sewing. If you make a mistake by mis-counting, cut away the stitches carefully in order to avoid snipping the canvas. A mistake spotted after only a couple of stitches can be undone by reversing the stitching process, with the needle still threaded, but take care to avoid splitting sitting thread. *Always* correct mistakes in Florentine work as soon as you spot them, otherwise the flow of the pattern will be interrupted and this will always be obvious. *Never re-use thread*. Cut your losses.

Line finders

Also called Chart Aids. (Available from Mary Gostelow.) These will help find your place on the chart, by the use of movable magnetized strips and an accompanying board.

Frames

If you are a beginner, always use a frame. It can help in many ways once you have mastered its handling. The canvas will be held at the correct tension for stitching. A rectangular tapestry frame, either fixed or rotating, is the most useful. Circular embroidery frames are not suitable, as they dent the canvas and are not strong enough to hold the canvas at the right tension.

If you are beginning a large piece of canvas work such as a stool cover, chair seat or firescreen, maybe you should invest in a flexi-floor frame. (Market Square UK have a good range.) These frames have adjustable elbows which enable you to position them at the angle best suited to you, and so prevent your back aching. The sizes of the hand frames range from 23cm (9in) wide to 90cm (36in). Floor frames range from 61cm (24in) to 90cm (36in) or wider. This measurement is crucial and should be wide enough to accommodate the width of the canvas cut to the required size. The length of the canvas will often be longer than the hand-frame drop (usually either 22.5cm (9in) or 30.5cm (12in)), but if you use an adjustable frame with rollers top and bottom, the canvas may be rolled away until required for stitching.

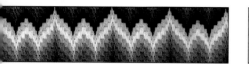

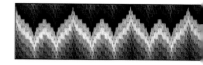

Chapter Four

PREPARATION & TECHNIQUES

Choice of colour

The two elements of Florentine work that combine to give it special quality are the shapes created by the pattern and the combination of colours. It takes time and effort to develop an awareness of which colours sit happily together on canvas, and which do not. Some needleworkers have an innate gift for making unusual, exciting, and unexpected colour choices; others may need help.

If you are intending to work several projects it is worth investing in a *manufacturer's shade card*. Choose colours that will harmonize or, if you prefer, contrast. If you see a 'natural' colour combination that pleases you, for instance in flowers, berries, fruits, walls, or stones on the beach, or on a design on china, porcelain, fabric or in a painting, bear it in mind for your own future projects. Television graphics and fashion magazines can also be a source of inspiration. Take risks, and try not to repeat yourself except by deliberate choice. Develop an awareness of the different density value of shades of any one colour. Keep dark, medium and light in mind always, and avoid using different colour tones of the same value together, because they blend together unsatisfactorily. Tone contrast is essential. Use a spare piece of canvas as a sampler (examplar) to work your

pattern and colour sequence, preferably the *same mesh as your project*, and keep this practice piece for reference. It can later be passed to a friend or to the next generation.

When choosing yarn colours, buy samples of each in skeins first, for two reasons: in order to work a small sample to test both pattern and colour combination, and to gauge more accurately the amounts you will require. Divide the required size of the finished product by the amount one skein covers on canvas, to determine how many skeins you need.

Do not hesitate to change any colour at this early stage, if you are not happy with one or more of your first choices. A stitched colour combination can look very different when compared to the skeins handheld like a posy in the shop. You will of course need to check that they harmonize or contrast with the other colours you are already using for furnishings.

When copying an old piece of Florentine work, look at the wrong side which, not having been exposed to sunlight and wear, will have remained more or less true to its original colours. You will be astonished how the colours on the right side have faded in comparison. Your taste will perhaps prefer the faded colours, if only because you have become accustomed to seeing the piece that way, but remember that sunlight, the old enemy of fabric, will in time fade your own work; choosing a colour combination somewhere between the old and the new might be the best solution.

If you cannot get the colours right for any project, go back to your needlework retailer. An interested specialist will always offer guidance, and sometimes a fresh eye is useful in helping you make a final workable choice.

Practical advice

To find the centre of the canvas, fold it in half lengthwise and press firmly with your hand along the crease on a flat surface. Fold the doubled canvas in half again in the opposite direction. The point at which the two folds intersect is the centre, and should be marked with an indelible water-proof pen or transfer pencil, or with ordinary hard black lead. Mark a hole, not a thread. Now mark the canvas top and bottom. Draw a line along the folds, vertically and horizontally, using a ruler. Some needlepointers prefer to tack along these guidelines with wool or cotton thread, but this can interfere with the surface stitching when with-drawn later. If you have marked these lines accurately and centre your first main establishing line of stitches, the pattern will sit correctly on the canvas, and the pattern will be uniform, if incomplete at either side, top and bottom.

Now draw the outline template of the required shape on to the canvas, centring it accurately, and checking that there is plenty of spare canvas on each side for the turning allowance.

Next bind all non-selvedges with 2.5cm (1in) masking tape. Place half the tape along the wrong (underneath) side of the canvas from the top edge down and press to stick securely. Fold the remaining half over on to the right (top) side of the canvas like a blanket ribbon. Repeat where necessary. This tape will prevent the canvas from fraying as you work, and will be removed before making up (see diagram 8). Alternatively, the edges of the canvas may be hemmed on a sewing machine using an interlocking stitch.

The canvas should now be attached to the frame braid. Mark the braid centre with an X top and bottom, and centre the canvas on these two marks. Use wool to tack the canvas on the frame braid, as it goes through both thicknesses more easily than cotton sewing thread. Use a blunt-ended tapestry needle for this. Adjust the wing nuts to bring the canvas to the correct tension. Do not have the canvas too tight, as it will distort when released from the frame.

Even though you will be anxious to start the decorative stitching, it is worth taking time to prepare at this stage, beginning and finishing off the basting stitches firmly to ensure the canvas will be held at the correct tension throughout its time on the frame.

You are now ready to begin work.

Threading the needle

It is not necessary to cut hanks of yarn into even lengths in Florentine work: just pull away as necessary or you will waste thread. The exceptions to this rule are:

a)   if you are working a linear pattern where each row requires a similar amount of thread, or

b)   when using perlé cotton.

Do not be tempted to use too long a thread, as woollen yarn will wear thin in the stitching. Thread should never be longer than 40cm (16in).

The end by which you pull away any yarn from the hank or skein should be threaded into the needle. All thread has a right and wrong way. Run your hand up and down each cut length: the correct way should feel smooth, and will sit better on the canvas. To thread the needle, double the end of the thread into a loop, and pull both sides of this loop along the shaft of the needle to ensure ease of threading. Pinch tightly together and insert into the eye. Knot the other end of the yarn.

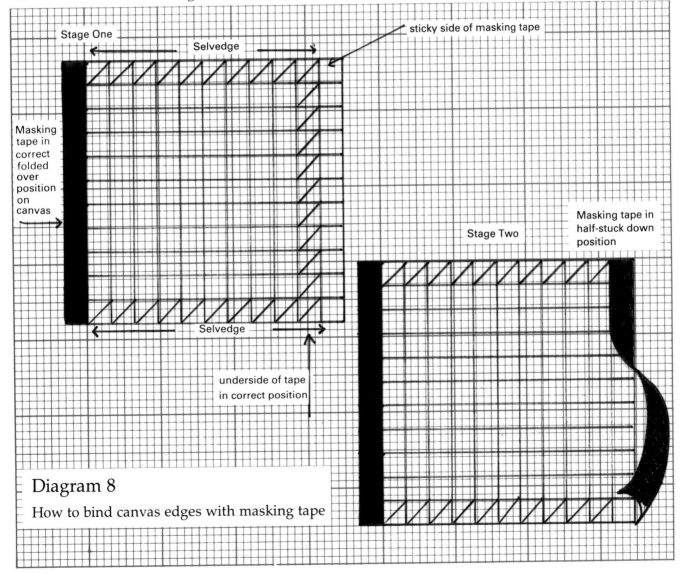

Stage One

Selvedge

sticky side of masking tape

Masking tape in correct folded over position on canvas

Masking tape in half-stuck down position

Stage Two

Selvedge

underside of tape in correct position

Diagram 8

How to bind canvas edges with masking tape

Stitching

1.   Remember that each hole of the canvas mesh is used twice (apart from the outside rows on the edge of the piece).

2.   Each stitch made is connected to its neighbours by the use of at least one common horizontal canvas mesh.

The order of stitching

The amount of wear to which the finished article is put will determine the order of stitching. In order to cover the *wrong side* of the canvas almost as completely as the right side, you will take the longest journey (on the wrong side of the work) from the end of one stitch to the beginning of the next. Check the wrong side of the work frequently as you sew. Remember always to change the direction of working a pattern after a *pivotal stitch* to make sure you are still covering the canvas completely.

However, a piece of work which will not undergo much wear can be more sparsely covered at the back, and you will require slightly less yarn. Florentine stitches have a natural bias or tilt as you move across the width of the canvas. In order to avoid a ribbed effect, work the canvas – after the main establishing row – from right edge to left on one row and back again from left to right on the following row.

Patterns in which several stitches lie parallel to each other in a block have a much denser covering than those where single stitches are stepped. Take this into account when choosing patterns: avoid their use on small articles such as eyeglass or scissor cases, purses, bookmarks and belts.

Work away from the central main establishing line up to the top limit of the canvas template, and roll it away on the upper part of the frame. Next work downwards from the central line so that your arm does not rub any completed work.

Begin each new length of yarn by knotting the end furthest from the needle's eye. Insert the needle from *front to back* into a position at least 5cm (2ins) away from where you will begin stitching and work towards the knot, taking care to couch it down on the wrong side as you progress. Finally, cut off the knot. Finish the thread off by weaving in and out of *the same coloured thread stitches* at the back of the work. It is very important to begin and finish off a length of thread with care, particularly because several meshes are covered by each stitch and the stitches may unravel if not secured firmly.

As you stitch, make sure that the yarn is not being pulled too tightly: it should stand proud of the canvas but not be too loose. If the canvas shows between stitches it is too coarse and you should change to one with a finer mesh, or use an extra strand of yarn in each needleful. Remember not to use too long a thread, as wool tires and coton perlé will lose its sheen.

Technique of stitching

In working each stitch there is a choice of which of two holes you should use first. Be consistent. When working parallel blocks in either direction from left to right or vice versa, take the longest journey. When travelling in a downward step, stab the needle through from the wrong side at the bottom limit of the stitch and complete by stabbing back out again from front to back at the upper limit of the stitch. The reverse is true when travelling in upward steps: stab through at the upper limit from back to front to begin each stitch and complete by using the lower limit of the stitch.

If you follow these rules consistently, your work will cover both right and wrong side of the canvas completely. Take care when changing direction at the *pivotal stitch* or stitches, where it is impossible to avoid one stitch leaving the canvas bare at the back. You can perhaps experiment for yourself when practising pattern sequences on your sampler. Start with a fairly coarse canvas, say #12 or #14 mesh and Paternayan (Paterna) wool, using 2 of the 3 strands of wool. Make a pincushion, a needlecase, a spectacle case or a cheque book cover. If you feel fairly confident with such undemanding patterns, use a much finer canvas, perhaps a #16 or #18, using either two or one strands of crewel wool, coton perlé or silk, to make any of the above small articles.

Working with coton perlé

Special care needs to be taken when working with coton perlé.

To prepare strands for working, take away the end papers, keeping the numbered paper tube on one side. Strip the yarn at the knot, holding the skein, and cut off a small length to tie into the number tube, which should be sewn to the side of the canvas, away from the working area. If you get into the habit of keeping a little of the numbered yarn for reference, you will save time if you need to purchase more supplies. Do this with all threads before beginning to stitch.

Next, cut the yarn from the skein in two. I keep my yarn in a white plastic key shape Gloria & Pat *My Floss Key-per* (pat pending) supplied by Dunlicraft Ltd (available at your needlework specialist supplier). Each key has room for about three full skeins of shades of any one colour and if knotted in correctly, the thread can be drawn away easily as you need it. Alternatively, use a wooden yarn holder.

An #18 Canvas will require one strand of coton perlé, and a #15 or #14 mesh three. Coton perlé is not recommended for coarse mesh canvases. When threading the needle with coton perlé it is important to make sure that all the strands run the same way in the needle, and are separated from each other. They tend to twist as you embroider and must be unravelled each time. Leave one hand free to smooth out the thread as you complete each stitch. Letting the needle drop from your hand occasionally in order to untwist thread can also help. Stitching with coton perlé takes time, but the finished result is worth extra trouble. Coton perlé work should always be dry cleaned.

Part Two

THE DESIGNS
& CHARTS

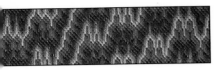 

Chapter Five

HINTS ON USING THE CHARTS

Good design

Most of us have the ability to recognize a good design. Perhaps we also can recognize bad design. The following list suggests some of the elements that should be present in the best designs.

Are the shapes well-proportioned and balanced?

Is there a sense of flow or movement?

Do the colours lie harmoniously: are there light, shade and subtlety?

Is there a cohesive sense of unity?

When designing your own patterns, try to keep these points in mind. Remember that the design should complement and enhance whatever it is intended to decorate.

The charts

The charts have been drawn in colour to make them easy to follow.

Count threads signified by the lines of the graph paper, *not* holes.

If you wish to enlarge a design, use a larger mesh canvas than on the worked sample; if you want a smaller design, use a finer mesh canvas.

There is always one central stitch, marked with a *c symbol*. On the main establishing line, when working out from the central stitch to the first edge *include* that stitch. When going back to complete the row, *omit* the central stitch. In subsequent rows you will work across the canvas from edge to edge, and proceed backwards and forwards.

A design repeat is indicated on the charts with this symbol ↑ —— ↑

A *pivotal stitch* is where the design changes direction. Care should be taken at these points to see that the back of the canvas is still being covered.

The *main establishing line* is the row you should work across the centre of the canvas, and should be stitched first. Follow the chart carefully when counting out this line and double check it before you proceed any further.

Chart 1

Spectacle case in basic Florentine stitch. I used a U-shaped made up case (from Et Cetera Supplies), lined in wine-coloured moiré cotton taffeta, piped in wine-coloured leather and zipped at the side.

Canvas: #15 canvas 25cm (10in)

Thread: Appleton's Old English crewel wools (five colours)

Size: made up case measures 15cm (6in) long at the centre fold by 7.5cm (3in) at the top when zipped up

Skill level: 1

Work the main establishing central row in navy blue. Work 21 rows plus 2 rows of irregular stitches, one at the top edge and one at the bottom curved edge to line up. Work in one piece and decrease at the ends of rows to accommodate the curves on either side.

Chart 1

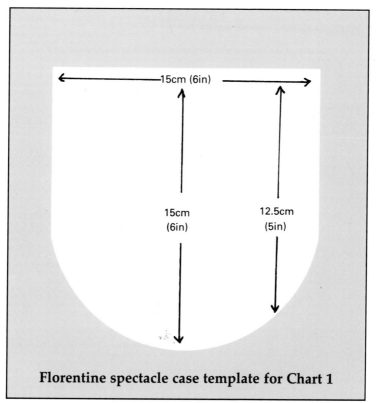

15cm (6in)

15cm
(6in)

12.5cm
(5in)

Florentine spectacle case template for Chart 1

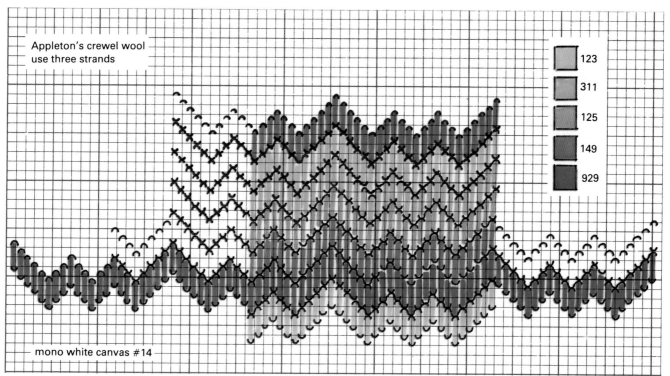

Appleton's crewel wool
use three strands

123
311
125
149
929

mono white canvas #14

Chart 2

Needlecase in varied stitch length rows of Florentine stitch. The example is lined with blue cotton chintz and has pinked leaves of white soft baby flannel for the needles.

Canvas: remnant of #15 white canvas 20cm (8in) × 15cm (6in)

Threads: stranded cotton or silk, 1 skein each of 6 colours

Size: made up, 15.5cm (6¼in) wide and 10cm (4in) long

Skill level: 1 if using stranded cotton; 2 if using designer silks

The worked sample shown was stitched in Pearsall's filoselle silk, but either stranded cottons or designer silks would also be suitable.

Work 20 rows of pattern and two edges of fill-in rows. Complete with two rows of tent stitch for the border.

Chart 2

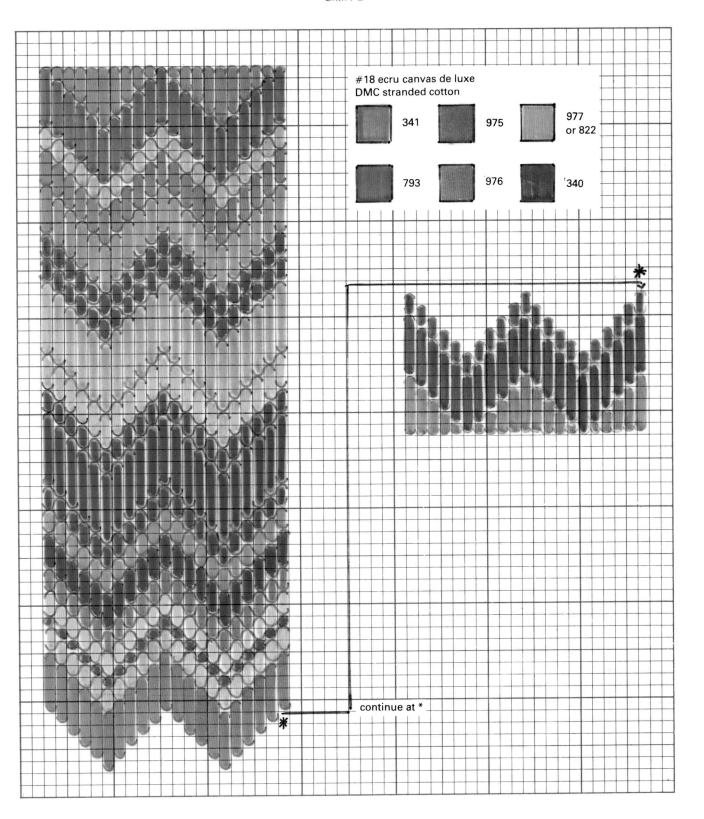

#18 ecru canvas de luxe
DMC stranded cotton

341   975   977 or 822

793   976   '340

continue at *

Chart 3

Paperweight, either oval or round, in stranded cottons using Hungarian background filling stitch bordered by Florentine stitch.

Canvas: #22 mono canvas for oval paperweight, oval-shaped canvas 16.5cm (6½in) × 14.5cm (5¾in) for round paperweight, circle-shaped canvas 14.5cm (5¾in) diameter

Threads: stranded cottons, 3 skeins, 1 of each colour

Size: oval 11cm (4½in) × 7cm (3⅓in)
round 9cm (3¾in) diameter

Skill level: 1

This basic pattern is designed to teach the use of these two stitches. Use four threads of the stranded cotton, saving two threads for the next needleful. Draw the outline of the glass paperweight in pencil on the canvas and fit the edges of the pattern to the required shape.

Work 26 rows (shaped) for the oval paperweight. Work 27 shaped rows for the round paperweight, fitting in a few stitches at the upper and lower edges as necessary.

Alternative colours are DMC stranded cottons 350, 353 and 355.

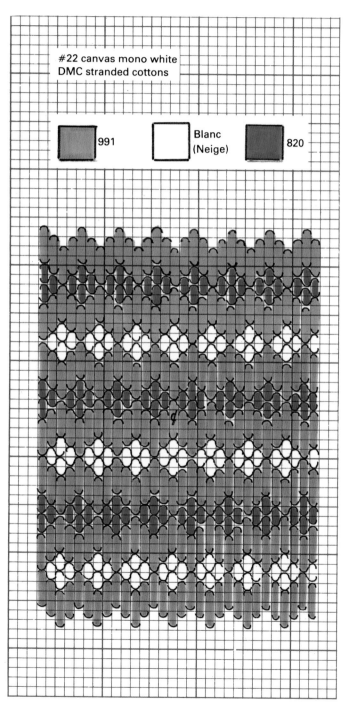

#22 canvas mono white
DMC stranded cottons

991   Blanc
           (Neige)   820

Chart 3

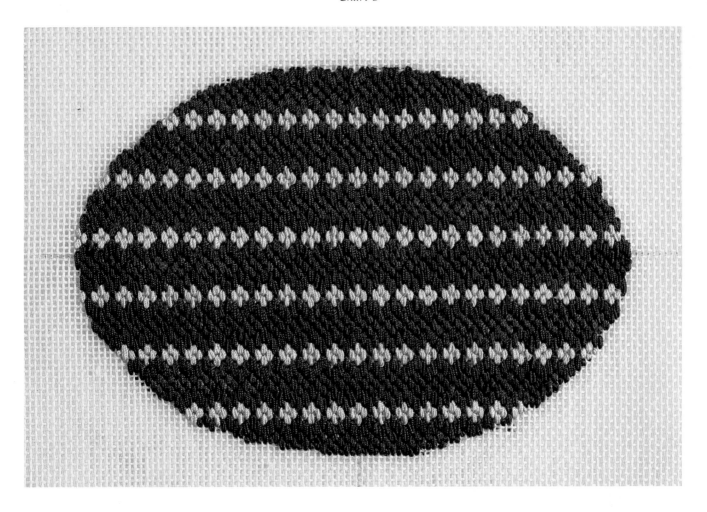

Chart 3

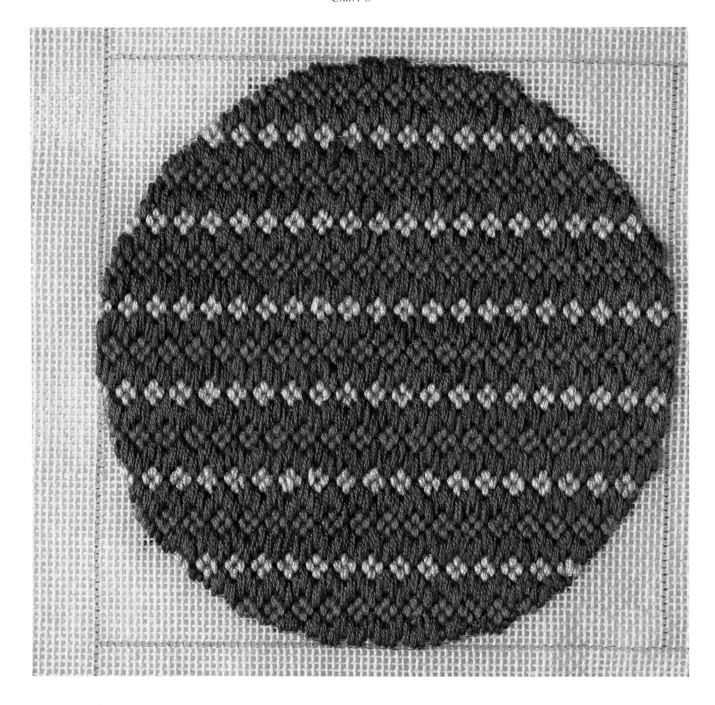

Charts 4 & 5

Suggested border designs; 5a and 5b are different
colour-ways for the same design.

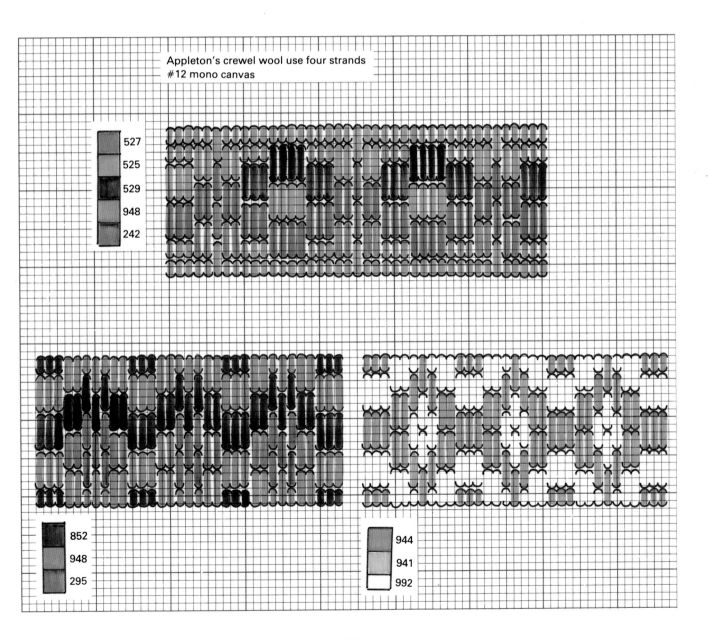

Note on mesh sizes

Having worked the first five charts and gained some experience, experiment with different mesh sizes. The two photographs here show how the size of a design is altered by being worked on a different mesh canvas.

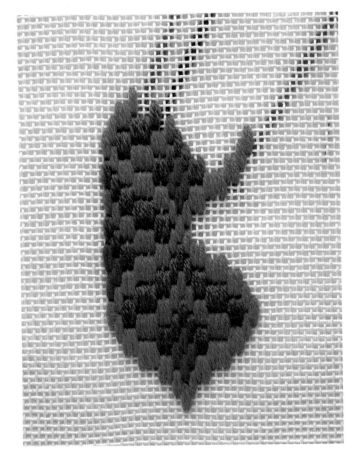

Chart 6

Minimalist Florentine peaked pattern in Florentine stitch.

Canvas: #14 white mono canvas 50cm (19¾in) × 39cm (15¼in)

Threads: Anchor tapisserie wool, 2 skeins of each of 7 colours

Size: finished design 34.5cm (13½in) × 33.5cm (13⅛in)

Skill level: 1

Begin with the white (401) yarn as the establishing row: the bottom limit of the central pivotal stitch of the higher peak is the centre of the canvas. Make sure that the yellow (290) row is complete at the upper edge of the canvas, as this colour dominates the design. After the central establishing row, work from left to right and then back on the following row from right to left to prevent stitches leaning on the bias.

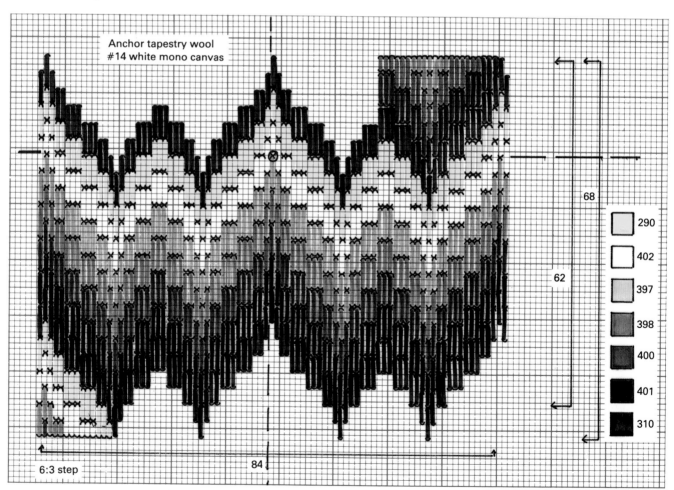

Chart 6

Chart 7

New Wave scatter cushion in DMC coton perlé no 5 and Gobelin stitch.

Canvas: #15 Zweigart mono de luxe écru 38cm (15in) × 33cm (13in)

Threads: DMC coton perlé, 10 colours (3 skeins 935 dark green background and one skein of each of the other colours)

Size: made up 28cm (11in) × 23.5cm (9¼in)

Skill level: 2 (1 if worked in wool)

Work 36 rows of pattern and interlocking background. Finish off with two rows of tent stitch all around the edges to act as guidelines for making up. The example shown was backed with a slubbed dusky pink matt cotton fabric, piped and zipped.

Each row has 174 stitches and just over half the pattern has been charted.

Chart 7

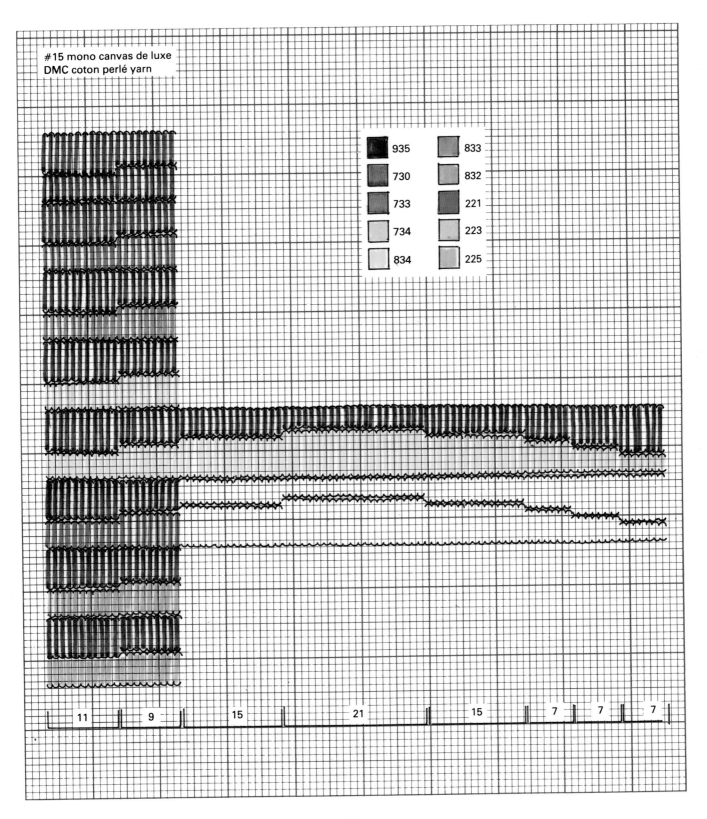

#15 mono canvas de luxe
DMC coton perlé yarn

	935		833
	730		832
	733		221
	734		223
	834		225

11   9   15   21   15   7   7   7

Chart 8

Pastel pincushion in diagonally-worked Florentine stitch.

Canvas: 25cm (10in) square remnant of #22 white mono canvas

Threads: DMC stranded cotton (use three strands), one skein of each of 10 colours

Size: 15cm (6in) square

Skill level: 2

Work ten patterns *diagonally* across the centre of the canvas in one column from the bottom lefthand corner to top right-hand corner. The central stitch is the first left-hand stitch on the sixth pattern up.

Work 23 rows, reducing the number of patterns on the rows at the top left and bottom right corners. Work out 12 patterns in 504 for the green border running horizontally along the bottom edge and repeat in the same way along the top border. Then work 25 rows in 504 to complete each of the side borders. Work three more rows of border using the colours at random. When working diagonally upwards from left to right, care must be taken that the beginning of each pattern repeat *moves up to the right* over four horizontal threads and one vertical thread.

The example shown was backed with *eau de nil* cotton chintz and stuffed with sawdust.

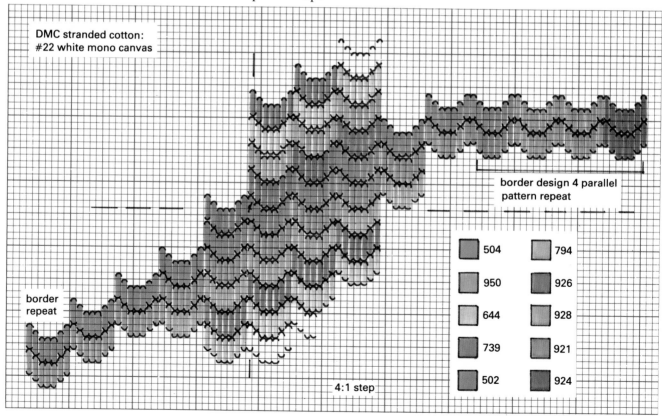

DMC stranded cotton:
#22 white mono canvas

border design 4 parallel
pattern repeat

border
repeat

4:1 step

504		794	
950		926	
644		928	
739		921	
502		924	

Chart 8

Chart 9

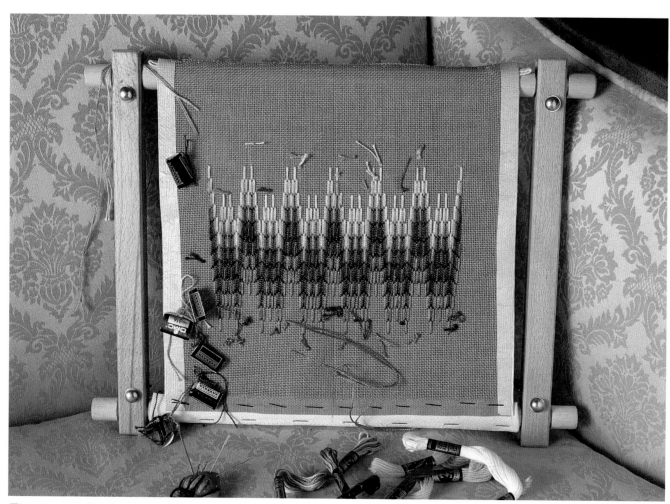

Zigzag peak design for a cushion cover in Florentine stitch.

Canvas: #18 mono Zweigart de luxe canvas

Threads: DMC coton perlé (use two strands) in 8 colours

Skill level: 2

When working this design, complete the row you are on before putting the work away, as it is otherwise easy to lose your place. Work up and down the pattern line of each row. Each successive stitch shares one horizontal mesh of the canvas with its neighbours. Colour 471 follows 778 on the upper half of the canvas. Colour 315 follows 471 on the lower half of the canvas.

This form of Florentine stitch is a good preparation for working Hungarian point.

Chart 9

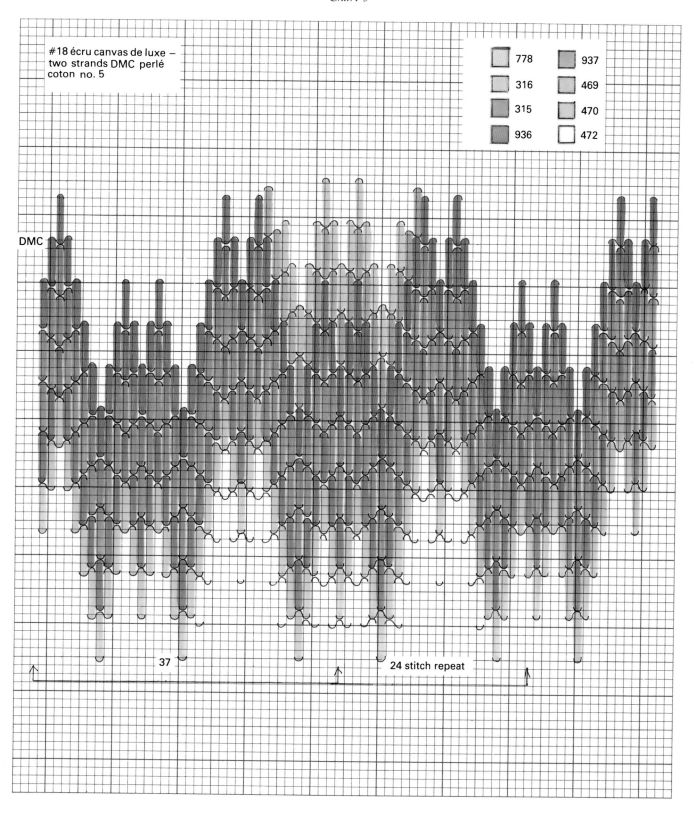

#18 écru canvas de luxe —
two strands DMC perlé
coton no. 5

778 937
316 469
315 470
936 472

DMC

37

24 stitch repeat

Chart 10

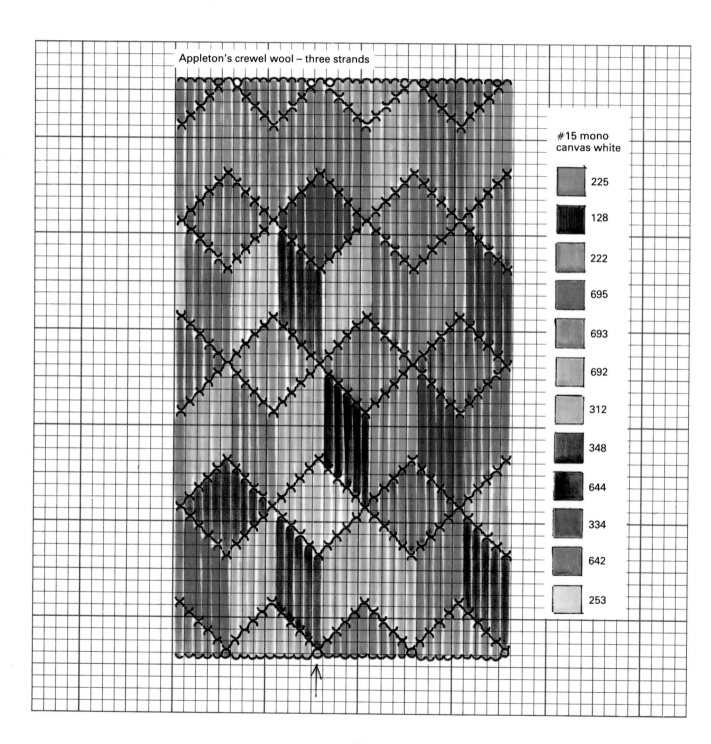

Appleton's crewel wool – three strands

#15 mono canvas white

	225
	128
	222
	695
	693
	692
	312
	348
	644
	334
	642
	253

Chart 10

a) Tumbling blocks design for a cushion cover in Florentine stitch.

Canvas: #15 white mono Zweigart canvas
Threads: Appleton's crewel wools (use two strands of wool) in at least 12 colours
Size: 21cm (8¼in) square
Skill level: 2

The colours were used at random. It is, however, important to be consistent about the relative placing of colour tones. The darkest tone of each colour block should be worked in the diamond shape. Work each block three times on the diagonal. The design will appear to jump and change direction if the placing of the colours is not consistent, as in the example shown. Notice that the chart has five stitches over eight threads and nine stitches in the diamond.

b) Cheque book cover in tumbling blocks in Florentine stitch (adapted from chart 10).

Canvas: #16 white mono Zweigart canvas 31cm (12¼in) square
Threads: Appleton's crewel wool (use two strands) nos 742, 745 and 749
Size: 22cm (9in) × 10cm (4in)
Skill level: 2

The example shown was worked in a made-up cover with blank canvas (from Et Cetera supplies). Work four stitches over eight meshes of the canvas in 742, then four more stitches in 745 and seven stitches in the diamond shape. The back of the cover is navy blue corduroy, piped in leather with brass clips at the corners. It is lined with chintz. Stitch good quality 2.5cm (1in) grosgrain ribbon inside to hold the cheque book in place.

Chart 10

Chart 11

Document case. Geometric flattened ogee-shaped design, worked in Gobelin and Florentine stitches.

Canvas: #16 white mono canvas 41.5cm (18½in) × 31cm (14½in)

Threads: Appleton's crewel wools, 2½ skeins 944, 3½ skeins 945, 3 skeins 947, ½ hank 946, ¾ hank 749

Size: 36.5cm (14½in) × 26cm (10½in)

Skill level: 2

The example shown was worked on a zipped document case made up with blank canvas ready to be worked (from Et Cetera Supplies).

Work the dark blue (749) shapes first in Florentine and Gobelin stitches. Then fill in the pinks.

Back the finished work with corduroy, and line the case with plain cotton chintz. This design would also be suitable for a cushion cover 46cm (18in) square or larger, or a chair seat cover.

Chart 11

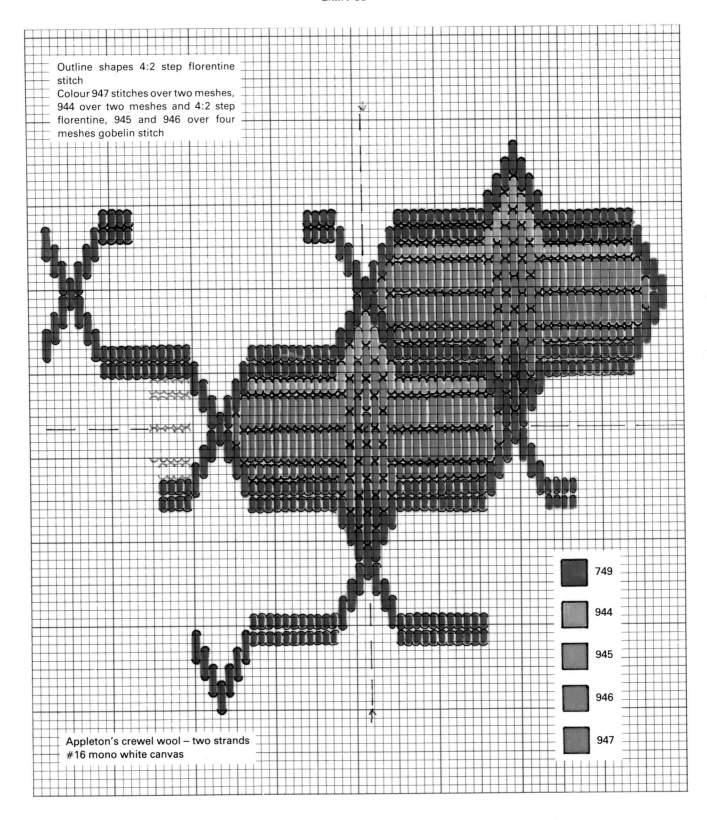

Outline shapes 4:2 step florentine stitch
Colour 947 stitches over two meshes, 944 over two meshes and 4:2 step florentine, 945 and 946 over four meshes gobelin stitch

749
944
945
946
947

Appleton's crewel wool – two strands
#16 mono white canvas

Chart 12

Design suitable for a handbag, or chair or stool seat. Florentine wave pattern in Florentine stitch.

Canvas: #12 white mono canvas

Threads: DMC coton perlé (use three strands), two skeins each of 7 colours for the handbag

Size: 38cm (15in) × 20cm (8in)

Skill level: 3

The design in the example shown was worked on a made up bag (from Casa Needlepoint).

When working with three strands of coton perlé, great care needs to be taken to ensure that each one lies flat and is not allowed to twist. Smooth the thread as you work each stitch. You can use crewel wool as an alternative.

Chart 12

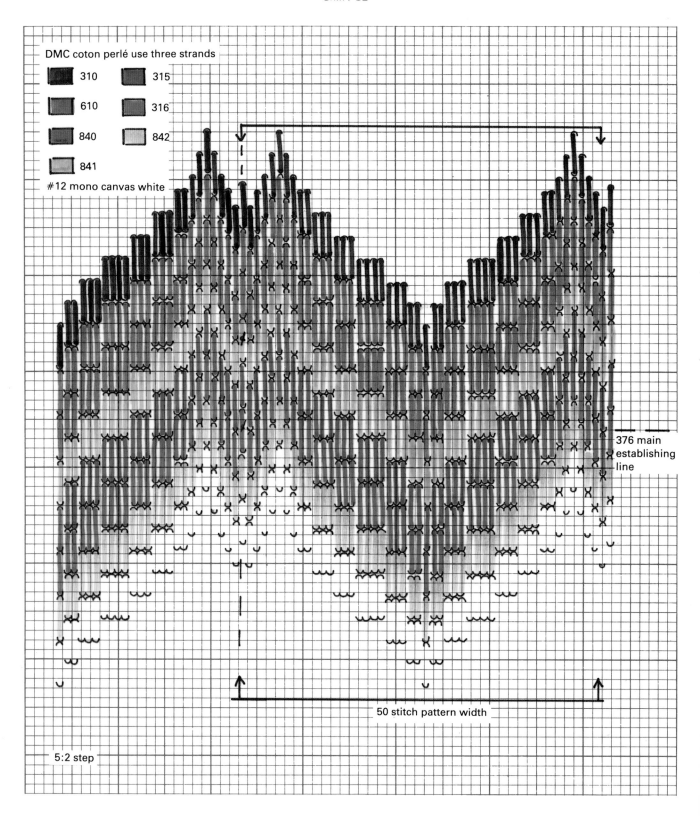

DMC coton perlé use three strands

310
315
610
316
840
842
841

#12 mono canvas white

376 main establishing line

50 stitch pattern width

5:2 step

Chart 13

Twin-peaked Florentine wave pattern in Florentine stitch suitable for a cushion cover or chair seat.

Canvas: #16 ecru canvas, 43cm (17in) × 34cm (13½in)

Threads: DMC coton perlé (use two strands)

Size: 34cm (13¼in) × 26cm (10¼in)

Skill level: 3

Complete one row at a time. It is best not to put the work away in the middle of a row in case you lose your way when you take it up again.

Work from the main establishing line in DMC 223 up to the upper limit of the required design size, filling in to the edge with shorter stitches where needed. Repeat from the main establishing line to the bottom edge.

The design below was worked in Appleton's crewel wool on an #18 mono canvas. Worked in coton perlé, the design would be far more subtle.

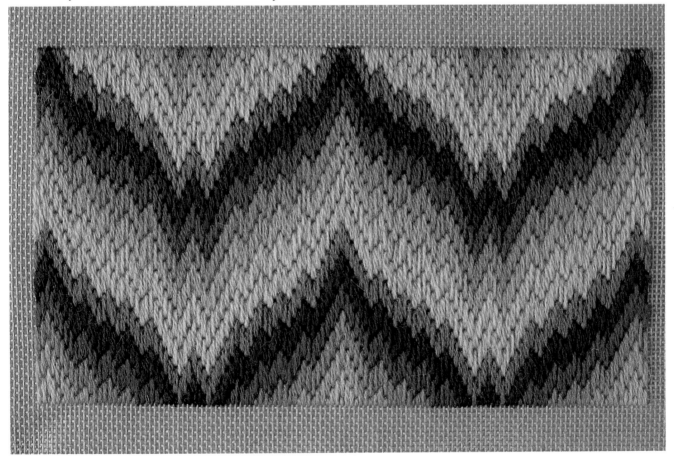

Chart 13

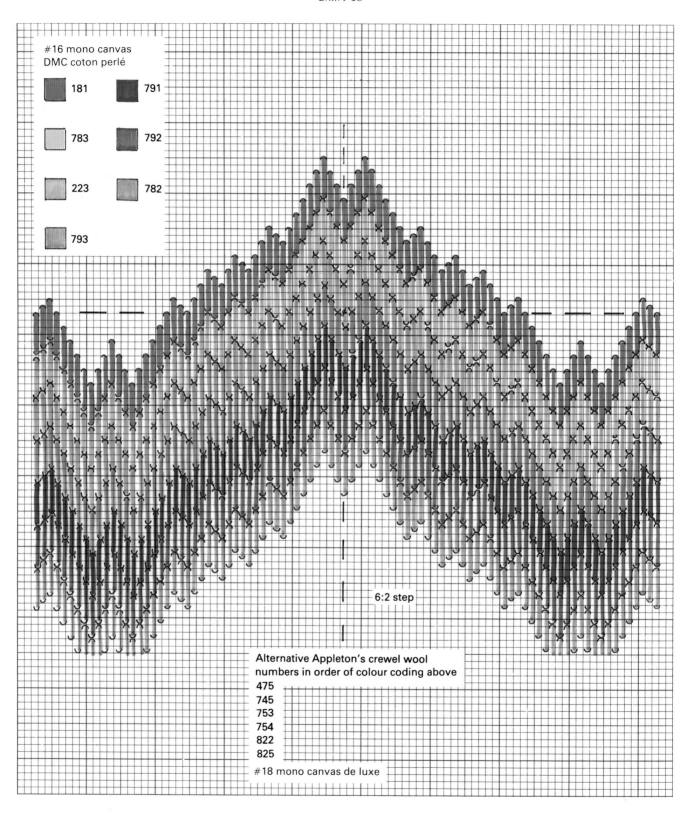

#16 mono canvas
DMC coton perlé

181   791
783   792
223   782
793

6:2 step

Alternative Appleton's crewel wool
numbers in order of colour coding above
475
745
753
754
822
825
#18 mono canvas de luxe

Chart 14

Intersecting ogee design in Florentine stitch for a cushion cover.

Canvas: #16 mono canvas de luxe ecru

Threads: Appleton's crewel wools, two 1oz hanks 159, one 1oz hank each of other colours

Size: 38cm (15in) × 30cm (13in)

Skill level: 3

Refer to the photograph of the completed sample cushion for help with placing the different colour combinations.

Work the dark blue outline ogee shapes first and next fill in the blue and beige ogees. It will become apparent that there is only one completely blue/beige ogee alternating with other ogees containing blue, pink and beige, in sequence. Once you have grasped the logic of the sequence you should not have any difficulty.

The example was backed with a heavy blue upholstery weight cotton fabric and self-piped to finish.

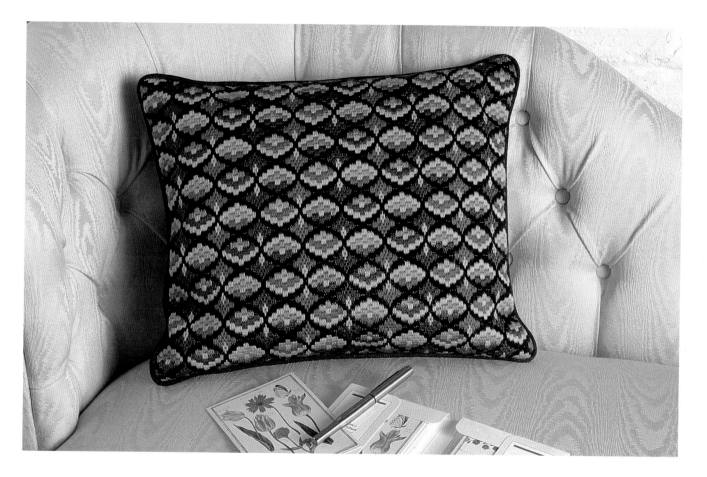

Chart 14

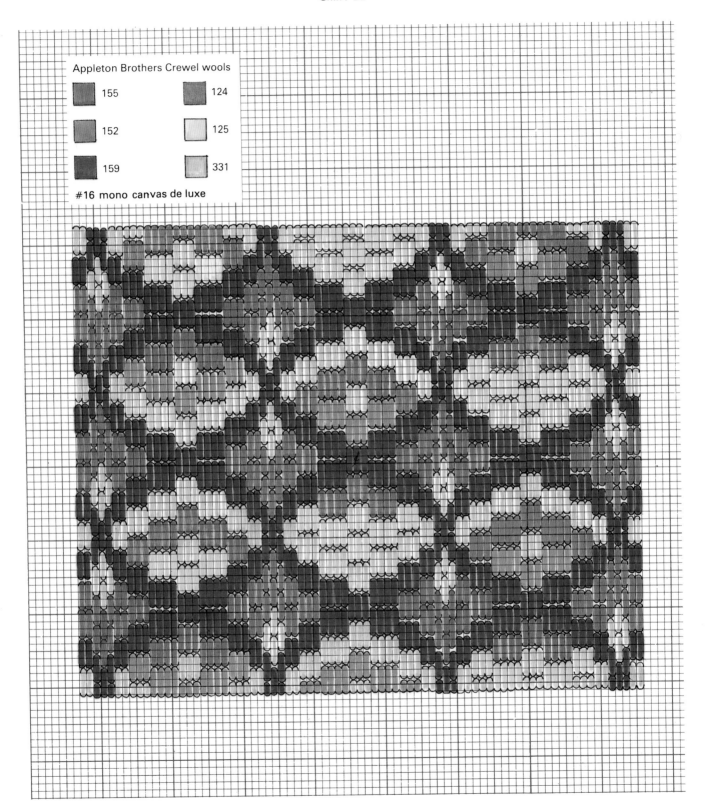

Appleton Brothers Crewel wools

155
152
159
124
125
331

#16 mono canvas de luxe

Chart 15

Flame pattern Florentine stitch design for a chair seat cover.

Canvas: #18 mono canvas de luxe

Threads: DMC coton perlé no. 5 (use one strand), 2 skeins of each of 7 colours

Size: 22cm (8⅝in) × 25.5cm (10in). Each individual pattern is 5.5cm (2⅛in) × 7.25cm (3in)

Skill level: 3

Work the trellis first in 934 coton perlé, then fill in the flames from the bottom of the ogee shape and work upwards. Work the top half of the canvas first and roll it away on the frame before completing the bottom half.

Chart 15

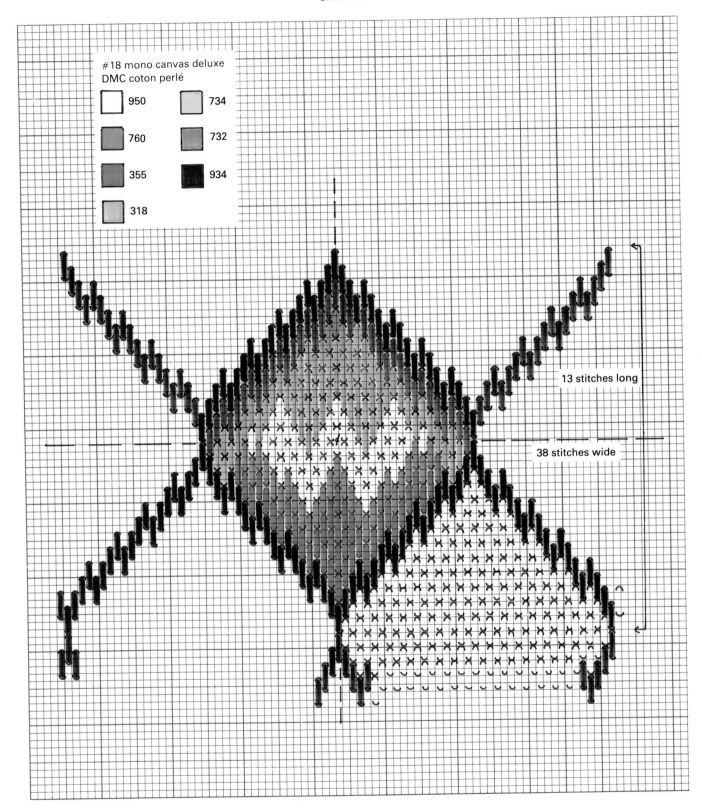

#18 mono canvas deluxe
DMC coton perlé

950
760
355
318
734
732
934

13 stitches long

38 stitches wide

Chart 16

Ogee design for a stool top, chair seat or cushion cover using either Appleton's crewel or tapestry wools, and DMC coton perlé no. 5 as highlight. Use three strands of crewel or one strand of tapestry.

Canvas: #14 mono canvas white, 50cm (19¾in) square

Threads: 1 hank 749 and 2 skeins each 821, 822, 823 and 874. 1 skein each crewel 744 and DMC perlé 3078 no. 5

Size: sample measures 41.5 × 38cm (16¼ × 15in)

Skill level: 3

Work outline shapes in 749 (darkest colour), first in Florentine stitch, 4:2 step. Take care with counting at this stage as each alternate ogee pattern shape across the canvas horizontally is larger than each of its neighbouring ogee shapes above and below.

One colour, 744, appears only in the larger ogee shapes. Finish off by working 3 rows of tent stitch on all four edges of the worked piece.

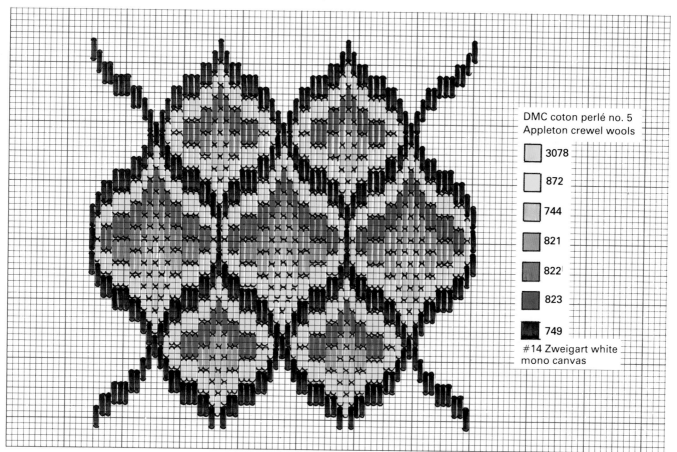

DMC coton perlé no. 5
Appleton crewel wools

	3078
	872
	744
	821
	822
	823
	749

#14 Zweigart white mono canvas

Charts 17 & 18

Cushion cover in intersecting circles. The example was worked in rayon threads purchased some 20 years ago and no longer available; I suggest that you substitute either coton perlé or silk.

Canvas: #18 white mono, ⅓m (13in)

Threads: DMC coton perlé no. 5 (use one strand), 1½ skeins of each of four colours

Size: 27.5cm (10¾in) × 23cm (9⅛in)

Skill level: 3

These two charts (17 and 18) are of the same pattern, but each has a different colour-way to demonstrate how the emphasis of a design can change radically by using different colour tones.

The example was backed with moiré silk, which complements the sheen of the thread.

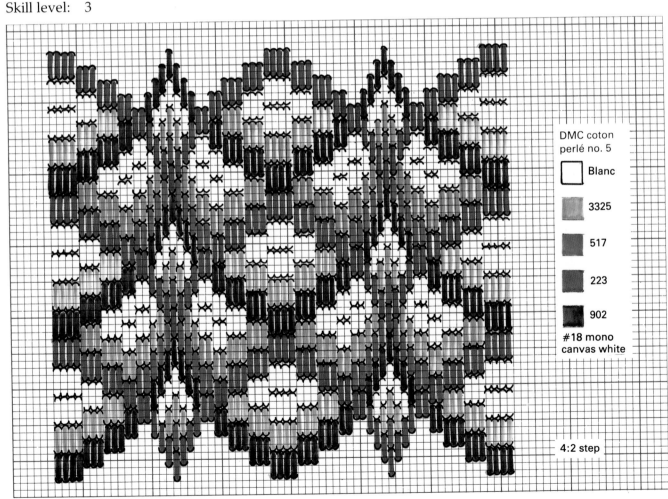

DMC coton perlé no. 5

Blanc

3325

517

223

902

#18 mono canvas white

4:2 step

#18 mono canvas white
DMC coton perlé

▦	3033	▨	939
▨	840	☐	762

4:2 step

Chart 19

Florentine-type geometric diamond pattern suitable for a cushion cover, a stool top or chair seat.

Canvas: #16 mono de luxe ecru, 40cm (15¾in) square

Threads: Appleton's crewel wools (use two strands)

Size: 28.5cm (11¼in) × 21cm (8¼in)

Skill level: 3

Notice that all the diagonal lines of the trellis running from canvas *top right* to bottom left use one uninterrupted colour each. The other diagonal lines, running from the top left to bottom right, change colour with one stitch at the intersection of the other diagonal.

Work the top right/bottom left diagonal trellis lines (three) first, then the other three trellis lines. Fill the diamond shapes from bottom to top later.

Chart 19

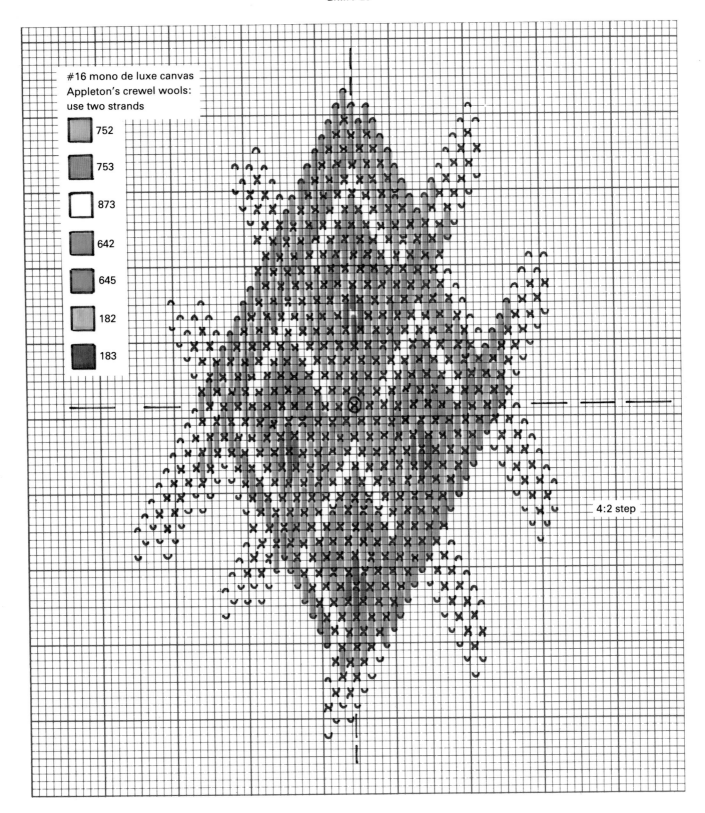

#16 mono de luxe canvas
Appleton's crewel wools:
use two strands

752
753
873
642
645
182
183

4:2 step

Chart 19

Chart 20

Bows cushion cover in Florentine stitch.

Canvas: #16 mono de luxe Zweigart écru canvas

Threads: DMC coton perlé no. 5 in three colours, 930, 932 and 977 as in photograph. 931 could be substituted for 977. Alternatively, use 451, 452 and 453 (muted lilac colours)

Size: 23.5cm (9¼in) × 14.5cm (5¾in)

Skill level: 3

This design also works well in Paternayan yarns.

Work the bows first and fill in the background later. Notice that the background pattern is irregular.

The example shown has a ruched frill using moiré cotton for the backing and trimming.

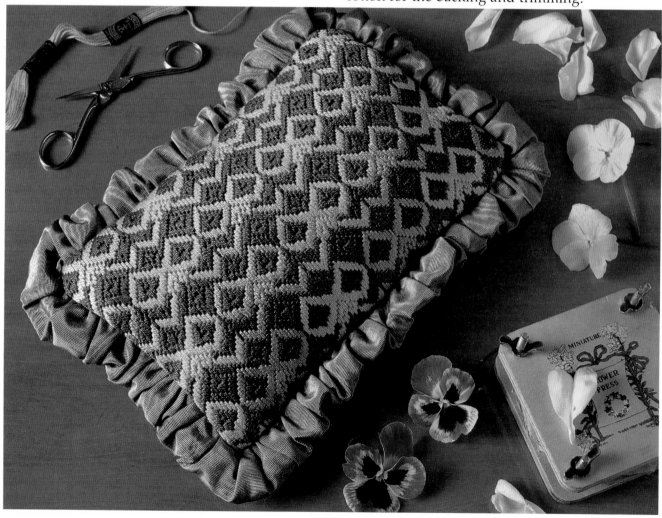

Chart 20

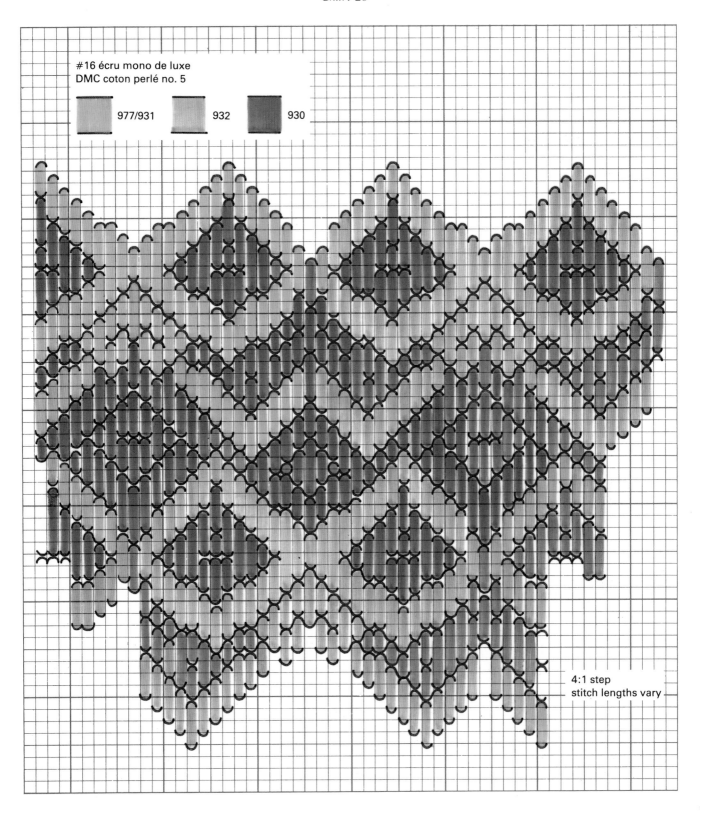

#16 écru mono de luxe
DMC coton perlé no. 5

977/931   932   930

4:1 step
stitch lengths vary

Chart 21

Florentine wave design cushion cover in dark blue with green coton perlé highlight.

Canvas: #14 mono de luxe, 50cm (20in) square

Threads: Appleton's crewel wools, one hank of each of 8 colours, plus two skeins DMC coton perlé no. 5 (use two strands)

Size: 36cm (14½in) square

Skill level: 3

This design is much more complicated to work than it appears at first because of the very slight differences between the darker wool colours. Work the coton perlé (587) as the main establishing line. The design length of nine patterns is 7cm (2¾in) deep and the finished cushion needs to have a fully-worked DMC peak at the top, as this is the dominant colour. Measure up accordingly.

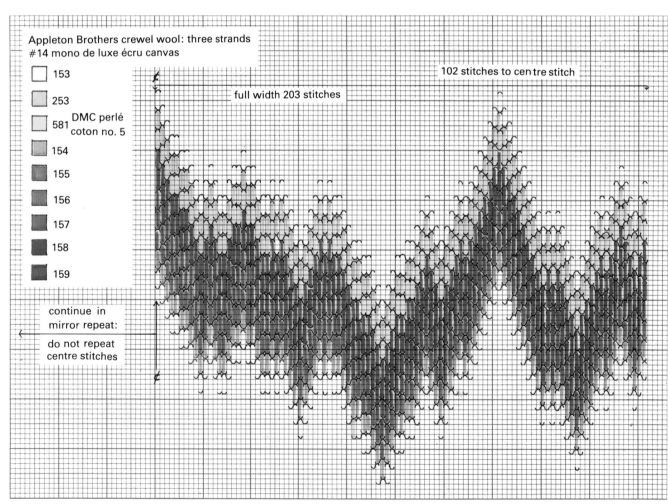

Appleton Brothers crewel wool: three strands
#14 mono de luxe écru canvas

153
253
581 DMC perlé coton no. 5
154
155
156
157
158
159

102 stitches to centre stitch

full width 203 stitches

continue in mirror repeat:

do not repeat centre stitches

Chart 21

Chart 22

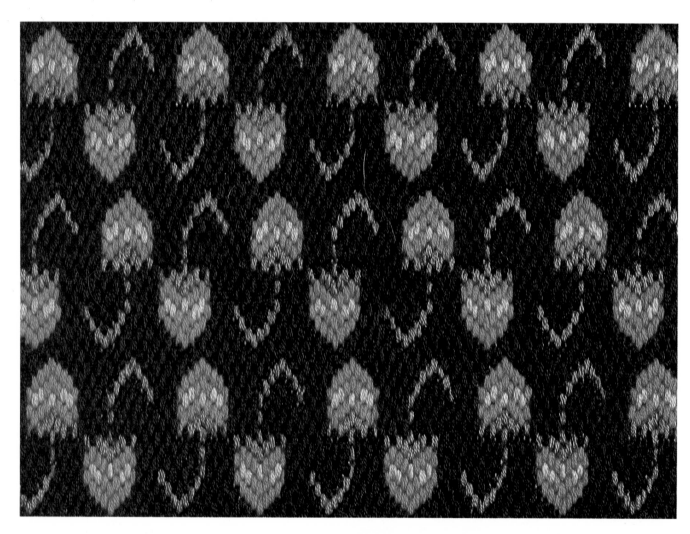

Strawberry pincushion worked in Florentine stitch.

Canvas: #24 yellow mono canvas, 20cm (8in) square

Threads: DMC stranded cottons, 2 skeins 939, 1 skein each of other colours

Size: 13cm (5⅛in) square

Skill level: 3

We did not include the border on the example shown, but it could be used on a cushion cover worked on #12 mono ecru de luxe canvas, in which case the strawberry design would work out twice the size of the design on the pincushion.

We used linen union to back the canvas. Make up with a 16cm (6¼in) square calico envelope stuffed with sawdust.

Chart 22

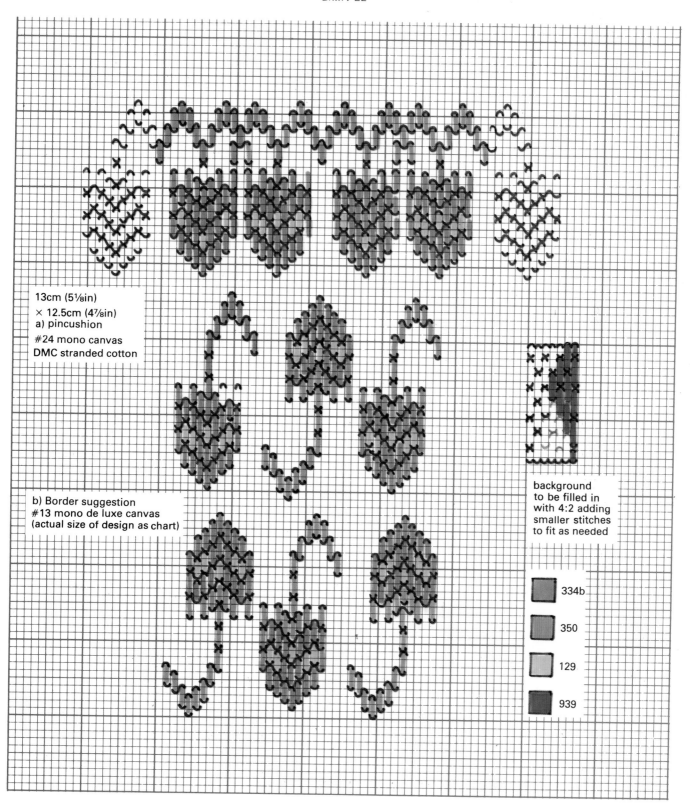

13cm (5⅛in)
× 12.5cm (4⅞in)
a) pincushion
#24 mono canvas
DMC stranded cotton

b) Border suggestion
#13 mono de luxe canvas
(actual size of design as chart)

background
to be filled in
with 4:2 adding
smaller stitches
to fit as needed

334b

350

129

939

Chart 23

Geometric outline with complicated trellis, suitable for a cushion cover or stool, in lilac blues.

Canvas: #14 white mono
Threads: Anchor tapisserie wools
Skill level: 3

We have shown a photograph of this piece of work in progress to demonstrate the trellis design only. Work this first and fill in the remaining shapes from the bottom of each shape upwards.

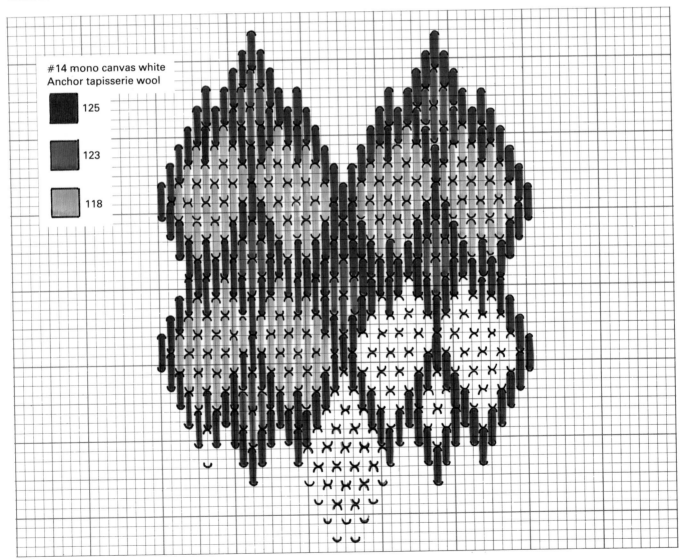

#14 mono canvas white
Anchor tapisserie wool

125

123

118

Chart 23

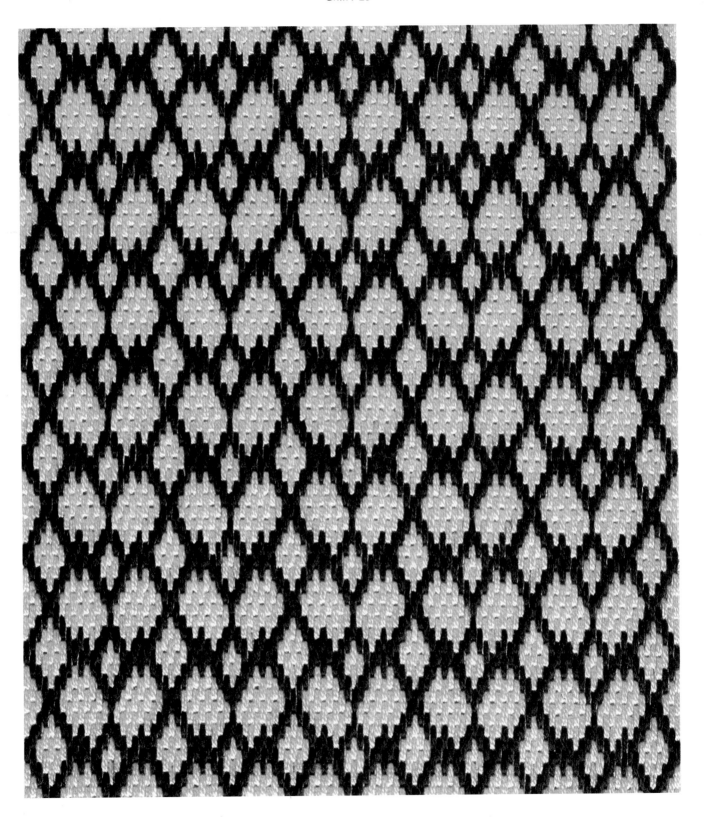

Chart 24

Hungarian point spectacle case. The pattern is also suitable for slippers.

Canvas: #18 mono de luxe écru, remnant piece 18cm (7in) × 44cm (17in)

Threads: Appleton's crewel wool, one skein of each of 7 colours

Size: 15.5cm (8¼in) × 11cm (4⅜in)

Skill level: 3

Work the case in one long piece. There are 15 pattern rows lengthwise and eight patterns across the width.

The example shown was made up with black moiré cotton and piped.

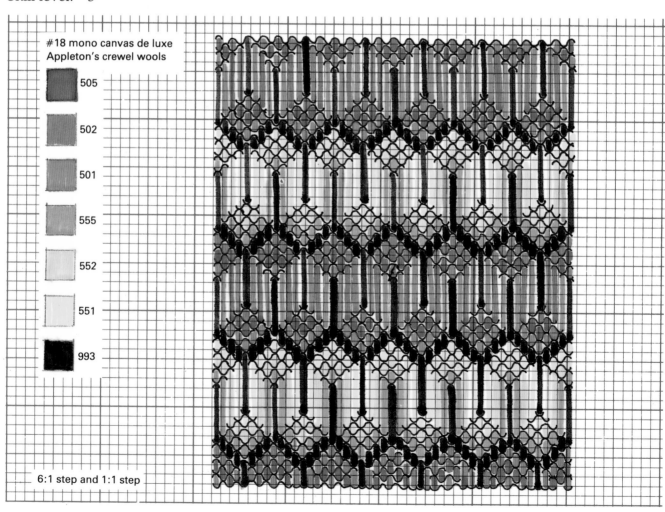

#18 mono canvas de luxe
Appleton's crewel wools

505
502
501
555
552
551
993

6:1 step and 1:1 step

Chart 24

Chart 25

Copy of an old Florentine flower pattern.

Canvas: #16 white mono canvas
Threads: Anchor stranded cottons, six colours
Size: 25cm (9¾in) square, including the border
Skill level: 3

An elegant chair with arms was worked by Mrs Christine Pope, who took this design from the original chair covering. I have charted the flower and background only, omitting the zigzag trellis.

The flower would look good surrounded by a simple diamond-shaped trellis or as a simple repeating pattern. The original chair has the flower pattern worked in two colour-ways.

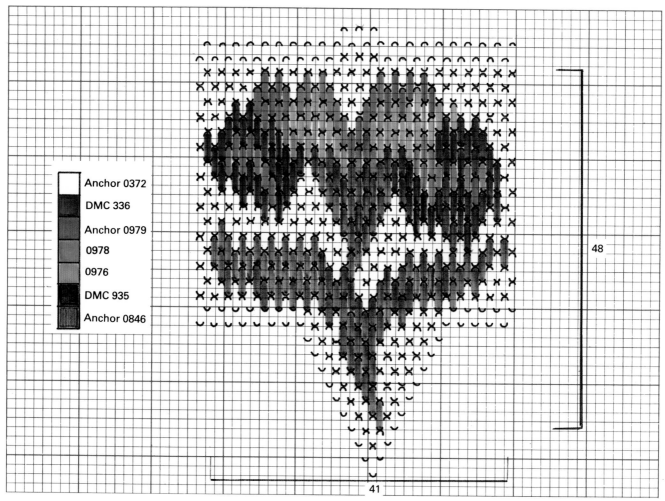

Anchor 0372
DMC 336
Anchor 0979
0978
0976
DMC 935
Anchor 0846

48

41

Chart 25

Chart 26

Hungarian point (stitch count two long, two short), for an armchair, adapted here for a long stool (see part title pages 38–9).

Canvas: #16 white mono canvas

Threads: Appleton's crewel wools, DMC coton perlé

Skill level: 3

This design is complex and should not be attempted until you are confident that you can work the simpler Hungarian point patterns.

The pattern needs a much deeper area than was possible on the stool, to show off the entire design. It has a swoop which is not visible here. It repeats every *fifth* line. Use whatever colours you are using at random, remembering that a very dark colour or the coton perlé can create useful highlights.

The pivotal directional change stitches require great care. It will be seen that the occasional peak is different. The pattern can be extended to be wider if necessary.

The checking line (each vertical) should read two short, two long. When working – from the centre, downwards first – remember to place each stitch immediately *below* the colour above, not at its side.

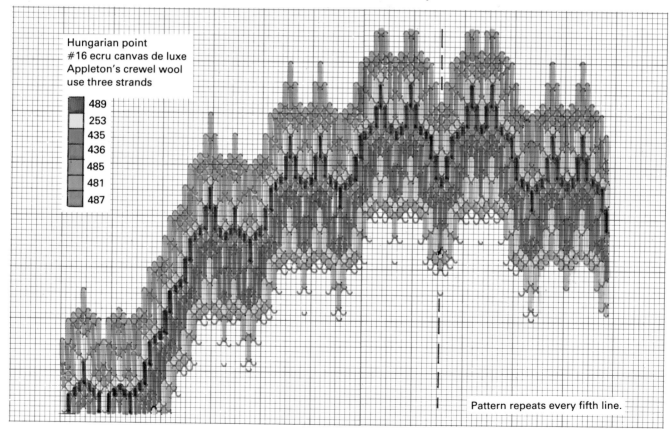

Hungarian point
#16 ecru canvas de luxe
Appleton's crewel wool
use three strands

489
253
435
436
485
481
487

Pattern repeats every fifth line.

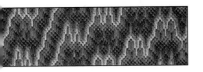

Chapter Six

FINISHING OFF & BLOCKING

Finishing off

When you have completed a design to the required template size, work a few extra rows in *tent* stitch all round the perimeter, to serve as a making-up seam guide. It will not be necessary to work these extra rows on upholstery, as you should have made adequate allowance on your template. Upright stitches *may* shrink vertically during the blocking process, so do make allowances for this when working the final rows.

Do not trim away the unworked canvas: it will be needed in the blocking process. There may be slight distortion of the work on completion, and the regular shape may have gone out of true. If this is the case, you will need to get it stretched (blocked) before making it up into the final form.

Blocking the Canvas

This is done by dampening and stretching (see diagram 9). It is best done professionally and any good needlework specialist will provide this service. It will greatly improve the look of the work. If you prefer to do it yourself, however, you will need:

1   A large piece of blocking (or insulating board). Do not use plywood because its colour may run into your work

2   An indelible laundry-marking pen (test that it will not run)

3   A ruler

4   Distilled water

5   Muslin pressing cloth

6   Non-rust tacks

To mark the board with guidelines to stretch along, draw horizontal and vertical lines at right angles across the surface of the board, keeping the cross lines 5cm (2in) apart.

Use a muslin cloth soaked in a solution of naphtha soap (if available) and distilled water and wring out, to dampen the canvas. Do not soak. Place the canvas work face down on the board so that the mesh is parallel to the marking lines. Lightly tack the corners. Tack along one side of the spare canvas along the guideline, pulling until the work is flat and smooth. Tack the opposite side, still pulling the piece into shape. Now tack the remaining two sides, beginning at the centre and working outward to the corners. Remove the original temporary corner tacks.

Allow the piece to stay in position until thoroughly dry. The greater the humidity in the atmosphere, the longer this will take. Avoid the use of wallpaper paste for stretching and blocking, as mites are attracted to it and have been known to destroy the work subsequently. The original sizing in the released by the dampening in the blocking process. Place the canvas and board in a cool airy situation away from strong sunlight or artificial heat. When completely dry, remove the tacks carefully and if necessary hold a steam iron away from the work to freshen up the threads.

Frame or make up into the finished article. Ask your framing specialist to choose a rebated moulding so that the work will not come into contact with the glazing. I do not recommend diffused or non-reflective glazing, as it takes all the texture out of the work, deadening it and making everything look like a framed photograph.

Take care never to hang either a framed piece of needlework or a made up wall-hanging on to a newly plastered or damp wall, as condensation will cause mould to appear on the work.

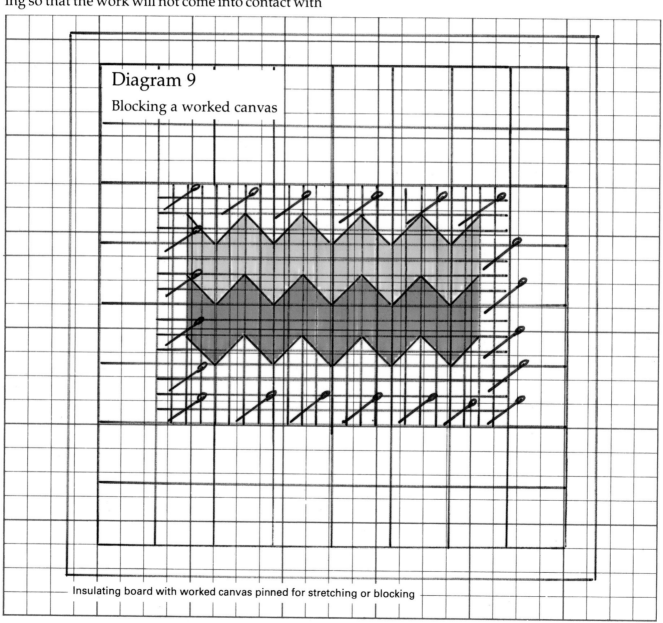

Diagram 9

Blocking a worked canvas

Insulating board with worked canvas pinned for stretching or blocking

Bibliography & notes

1. Rozsika Parker, *The Subversive Stitch*, The Women's Press, 1984
2. Gill Spiers and Sigrid Quemby, *A Treasury of Embroidery Designs*, Westbridge Books in arrangement with Bell & Hyman Limited, 1985
3. Dorothy Kaestner, *Four Way Bargello*, and *Needlepoint Bargello*. (Charles Scribner's Sons)
4. Isaam El-Said and Ayse Parman, *Geometric Concepts in Islamic Art*, The World of Islam Festival Publishing Company Limited, 1976 (Foreword by Titus Burkhardt)
5. Kamaladevi Chatthopadaya in *The Arts and Man*, United Nations Educational, Scientific and Cultural Organisation SHG, 1969, 68/037/A
6. Guy Le Goff, *L'Ornement Liturgique Tridentinen Anjou* (extract from the Catalogue for an exhibition in 1986 at Abbaye de Fontevraud, 303 Recherche et Creations No. 10 44047 Nantes)
7. Virginia Churchill Bath, *Needlework in America*, Mills & Boon Ltd (first published 1979 Viking Press/A Studio Book)
8. *Mary Gostelow's Embroidery Book*, Penguin Books, 1982
9. Lanto Synge (General Editor), *The Royal School of Needlework 'Book of Needlework and Embroidery'*, Oregan Press Ltd, 1986
10. Fernand Braudel, *Capitalism and Material Life*, Fontana/Collins. Translated by Miriam Kochan
11. Thérèse de Dillmont, *Encyclopedie des Ouvrages de Dames*, Paris Librairie Ch. Delagrave
12. Barbara Snook, *Florentine Canvas Embroidery*, Batsford, 1967

Other titles for further reading

1. Barbara Müller, *Florentine Embroidery*, Thorsons Publishing Group, 1989
2. *A Practical Guide to Canvas Work* (from the Victoria & Albert Collection) Unwin Hyman, 1987
3. Pauline Fischer and Anabel Lasker, *Bargello Magic*, J. M. Dent & Sons Ltd, 1972
4. Elsa S. Williams, *Bargello (Florentine Canvas Work)*, Van Nostrand Reinhold, 1967
5. Adolph S. Cavallo, *Needlework*, c. 1979 Smithsonian Institution

Index

Bargello 12, 13, 18
blocking the canvas 29, 93–4
border designs 49

canvas
    binding edges 34, 35
    blocking 29, 93–4
    finding the centre 34
    mesh size 28, 29
    preparation 34
    sizes 27
    types 27
carnation design 12
chair/stool seat 65, 66, 71, 73,
    77, 86, 90, 92
characteristics of Florentine
    work 12–13, 14
charts, understanding 25, 41
cheque book cover 61
colours
    choosing 32–3
    tones 12, 26, 32
copying Florentine work 32–3, 90
coton perlé 30, 37
cottons
    soft 29
    stranded 30
cushion covers 54, 58, 61, 67,
    69, 73, 74, 77, 80, 82, 86

design
    elements 40
    enlarging 41
    historical influences on 12,
      14, 16
    suitability 25

design size, calculating 28
document case 63
dye lots 30

Eurasian needlework 14

finishing off 93
frames 31
framing articles 94

handbag 65
historic examples of Florentine
    needlework 15, 16

interlock canvas 27
Islamic influences on design 14

line finders 31

mistakes, correcting 31

needlecase 44
needles 29, 30

origins of Florentine
    needlework 13, 15

paperweight 46
patterns
    bows 81
    choosing 25–6
    flame 72
    Florentine peaked 52, 68
    Florentine wave 66, 68, 82
    geometric diamond 78
    intersecting circles 74, 76

ogee 64, 70, 73
strawberry 85
trellis 86
tumbling blocks 60
zigzag peak 59
Penelope canvas 27
pincushion 56, 84
pivotal stitch 36, 37, 41
PVC canvas 27

scissors 30–1
silk yarn 30
slippers 88
spectacle case 42, 88
step 25
stitches
    brick 13, 20, 21
    diagonal Hungarian 19, 20
    Florentine 20, 21, 43, 45, 46,
      52, 56, 59, 60, 64, 66, 68, 70,
      72, 73, 81, 82, 85, 86
    Gobelin 21, 55, 64
    Hungarian 18, 19, 20, 46
    Hungarian point 16, 22–4, 88,
      92
    Old Florentine 19, 20
    straight 13
    tent 21
stitching
    order of 36
    technique 36–7

threading the needle 35
threads and yarns 29–30

wallet 77
wool yarns 29–30